No. 1

The
Little
Review

The Little Review is edited, designed and published by Tristram Fane Saunders in York, England. It is printed in the UK. The text is set in Adobe Jenson, created in 1996 by Robert Slimbach, with roman characters based on a 15th-century typeface cut by Nicolas Jenson, and italic characters based on the 16th-century work of Ludovico degli Arrighi. The inner covers of this issue feature a still life painting by Peter Binoit (c. 1590-1632).

Enquiries: editor@thelittlereview.co.uk

ISSN: 2977-8255 | ISBN: 978-1-0684443-0-2

Marx, Duck
& the boneyard

Names are hard work.

A lazy species, largely happy to ride on our writers' coattails, we literary magazines will steal any old name if it saves the trouble of thinking up a new one. So we rummage in the boneyard of dead mags. Breezing past a few mouldering headstones –

> *The London Magazine,* died 1785
> > *The Criterion,* d. 1939
> > > *Poetry London,* d. 1951
> > > > *The Fortnightly Review,* d. 1954

– we move on quickly, hoping to prise a good title from the grip of a grand old quarterly, like a ring from the grave of some deposed duke. Bolder mags would use that ring to proclaim themselves the heir – *The Criterion* is dead! Long live *The New Crite-*

rion! – while a real weirdo might even claim to *be* the old duke, dead yet walking – oh, *is* this birthday your 160th, *Fortnightly*? – were you *really* founded in 1732, dear *London Magazine*? – but such questions are not ours to ask. We don't know anything. We were born yesterday.

Why all this witter about names? They're not so very important. Good writing is good writing, regardless of the name it appears under; to prove our commitment to this idea, nothing we publish appears beneath the name of its author. We would like readers to consider every piece on its own terms – rather than flicking through the mag looking out for familiar names (which is, we are told, how less interesting magazines are read). Instead of names, there are discreet initials, decoded by a key at the back.

Still, recycling an old name can have curious side-effects. The flavour of the late magazine sometimes clings to its title, just as the ring retains a faint taste of the duke's decomposed finger. That may be the case here. We are not *The Little Review* (b. 1914, d. 1929) nor were we meant to be. But if a ghost haunts our pages, we hope it's Margaret C Anderson, the radical editor who made that magazine a safe haven for anarchists, feminists, Dadaists, *Ulysses* and Elsa von Freytag-Loringhoven. Her standards were exacting: once, when she felt the submissions hadn't been strong enough, she printed a dozen blank pages. We can't match her brilliance, but we admire her maverick attitude. Her first editorial declared that her magazine (like this one) was 'neither directly nor indirectly connected in any way with any organization, society, company, cult or movement', leaving it free to 'enjoy that untrammelled liberty which is the life of Art'. Sound words.

Elsewhere in that first issue, one piece argued wittily (and anonymously) that her as-yet-unpublished magazine had *al-*

ready got Rupert Brooke completely wrong. This is the kind of thing we like. We *want* to contradict ourselves. You don't have to be large to contain multitudes.

Reading a century-old magazine is a pleasant reminder of that now-endangered species, the blunt review. A typical two-sentence dismissal in the old *Little Review* introduced one novel as 'the kind of sweet, gentle love story' that publishers (not readers) seem always to want, before concluding: 'We searched in vain for just one page to hold our interest.' Margaret, this new *Little Review* wants to hold your interest.

Too many magazines are dull. Boredom is the enemy; as Baudelaire wrote, it wants to 'make the earth a shambles / and swallow the world in a yawn'.

We would much rather be wrong than dull.

And when we *are* wrong, we'd like *you* to set us straight. If you have an opinion about anything in these pages, share it with us (mailbox@thelittlereview.co.uk). We welcome letters. We would also like to see our mailbox filled with news, blessings, threats, event listings, information about forthcoming publications, intriguing quotations you've found in old books, and – above all – gossip.

Speaking of which: one poet recently made the mistake of confiding in us after a couple of pints, clutching our arm like the Mariner, reliving a painful tale. Our memory is hazy, but we think his story went like this: once, long ago, in a more innocent and barbaric age, when dinosaurs roamed the earth and reviewers occasionally said what they thought, this poet reviewed a book of poetry for a now-defunct small magazine. The poet wanted to be honest, so the review pointed out the obvious: the book was no good.

The man responsible for this book was a well-known figure in publishing back then, and still well-known now (but, we hope, not *quite* so thin-skinned). He wrote a series of angry letters complaining about the review to various people, including more than one missive to the poet's place of work. 'Are you aware,' he asked, 'that you have somebody on your staff who is *bringing poetry into disrepute?*'

Poetry – in disrepute! A frightful idea. Thank heavens Baudelaire, Behn and Byron aren't alive to hear of it. We share this story not for its historic interest, but by way of a parable. We do not care about the reputation of Poetry, except to lower it; we are interested in poetry, not Poetry. We have a great deal of respect for poems; we have none for poets, although their lives are often amusing. We *want* to bring poetry into disrepute. Our critical and artistic role models are Groucho Marx and Daffy Duck.

Help us in this noble quest. Send reviews, essays, poems, anything you like, so long as it's 'splendid and disreputable' – as Martin Bell wrote in his 'Ode to Groucho'. Like the guy behind the cigar, we want to 'Be talkative and shabby and / Witty; bully the bourgeois; / Act the obvious phoney' and raise a thick, painted eyebrow at 'an age of ersatz heroes'. Surprise us. Goad us. Delight us. Baffle us. We stand before you like John Ashbery's Daffy Duck – 'disingenuous, intrigued, inviting more'. 🐝 **TFS**

Contents

Fiction

'Furious desperation burned inside him'

All Women One

When Anne-Marie walked into Werner's room, he laid his carving to one side, brushed shavings from his knees, and turned his young, pale face towards her. The dark eyes held a hint of gratitude. It was as touching as the gaze of an orphan, or someone lonely and sick. Anne-Marie probably didn't notice because she was used to it. But she smiled and then, with naive fascination, examined the work he'd interrupted.

She crunched a few curled wood-shavings between her delicate fingers and asked: 'Virgin Mary?'

With a nod, Werner gave his usual reply: 'Virgin Mary.'

Occasionally, a Station of the Cross, or an alcove beside a great door, gave rise to an order for a Saint John or a Saint Lawrence. And sometimes a Saint Nicholas would be needed, encircled by the inscription 'Patron Saint, Preserve us from the Perils of Water'; or even a Saint Giles, with the inevitable epigraph 'Protect us by your Grace from Mange.' But they would be special orders, and Werner didn't get many of those because of his illness. So he mainly carved whatever he wanted, and these days it was Madonnas. Big, proud, maternal ones, cradling the chubby Christ Child in the rich folds of their sleeves. Or small helpless ones, totally exhausted and longing to be relieved of their tiny Redeemers. They sagged under the burden of multitudinous blessings which they had to carry, and could not stop wondering how they came to be mothers in the first place. There again, there were others, under tall, broad crowns, with arms open in boundless generosity. And there were more – with arms prudishly folded over their chests, whose eyelids always drooped owing to the weight of their perpetually downcast gazes. And, last of all, came those who cried out to be painted; they got red cheeks and very red lips – and they looked much healthier and more splendid in no time. But in one respect they were all alike: they were all radiant with gratitude to Werner, without whom they could never have existed. And, if only people had knelt before them, they'd have mustered that energy together to help the young man regain the use of his legs, paralysed since he was 16. But the trouble with not being ordered was that most of the Madonnas had to keep themselves to themselves in the attic, waiting for who knows what, and it never occurred to them that they might be capable of miracles, or indeed that teamwork might improve their chances of miracle-working.

The townsfolk couldn't believe that Werner didn't tire of carving Mary after Mary, and the oldest ones shook their heads in astonished disapproval. It was sacrilegious, they thought, for how could anyone know what the Virgin Mary looked like, least of all Werner, who couldn't even get to church because of his lameness. Anne-Marie alone seemed not to be surprised. It seemed perfectly right to her, when she thought back to that good little boy, with whom she'd wandered through the dreary meadows on the edge of town. That was before his illness. He was pious and sensitive then, although she was a little scared of a certain shyness, and a sort of shiftiness about him. At the same time, she was touched by his helplessness, and attracted to it. If they weren't talking, and hadn't found any flowers, there'd often be a song on his lips, soft with the weight of desire, and no-one knew where he'd learnt it. And when the red sun went down behind the willows, he'd burst into tears as if someone he loved, some real person, had just died. That was when both of them were children. And Anne-Marie couldn't see any great inconsistency between him sobbing as evening fell, and his carving of Madonnas, particularly now that he was ill. So she didn't feel there was anything odd about spending time with Werner. Sitting with him now that he couldn't walk seemed as normal to her as crossing the fields with him when he could. And if she found it moving to stare at the wooden saints, it was no odder than him being moved to tears at sunset. In him, she still saw that strange playmate who wanted her pity and her smile; sometimes she dreamed of his deep, suffering eyes, and of his hands – as white as a young girl's – which, as the sun went down, always seemed poised on the point of dispensing blessings.

These were the thoughts that ran through her mind as she sat with the sick man; and then, tilting her head with its thick chestnut hair, she clasped her hands in her lap, and gazed into Werner's face as if it were a vast landscape.

'What's the matter, Anne-Marie?'

Coming to, she said simply 'I'm thinking.'

'What are you thinking, Anne-Marie?'

'I'm thinking... Are many people always ill like you?'

'I'm afraid there are all too many, Anne-Marie.'

'Oh! So, for them, the world, the forests and the big cities full of strange and marvellous things don't exist? They never see any of it.'

'They dream about them, Anne-Marie.'

She said nothing. She felt ashamed.

Once, at a time like this, at dusk, Anne-Marie said 'You know, I often wonder whether you yourself pray to the wooden Virgins you've carved?'

The sick man smiled thinly, 'I just make them. That's my prayer.'

Anne-Marie thought a moment before speaking, as if to herself, 'How do you imagine Mary? Why like that exactly? Has it to do with some lovely picture you once saw?'

'I don't know. A picture or a dream. But she's always before my eyes. She's like longing.'

Then the girl asked 'Which of them is most like her?'

Werner replied with his eyes closed 'Every one of them is the Virgin. If you give grace, mercy, strength and devotion to one, you give it them all, and so they're all like her. I have to carve her again and again to encompass all her goodness and trust. All those I've made, and those that are to come, they are all... her. That's how much I love her.' He stretched out his arms solemnly as though he'd seen a vision.

Then Werner leant forward, grabbed the figure he was working on, raised it up into the evening light and chuckled 'Maybe I'll succeed eventually: one woman for all women.' He heaved a great sigh. 'And that will be for you, Anne-Marie.'

A mischievous look crossed Anne-Marie's face, and she burst

out laughing 'For my wedding.'

'What do you mean, your wedding?' Werner's voice was strange and hoarse with dread.

Anne-Marie replied seriously 'Because it's a celebration.' And suddenly, she felt very afraid.

❧

So, now, Anne-Marie had to have a Madonna. Every morning, Werner dragged himself on his crutches into the far end of the attic to find the right wood. But none was right, and so he sat there in a freezing corner, worn out by the climb and the searching. Slowly, he'd peruse the massed gathering of Marys, all of them so sad never to have stood in front of a child in prayer, or a candle lit on a Saturday. But Werner's mind wasn't on these dusty, good-for-nothing saints. His only thought was of Anne-Marie getting married – she must have a Madonna as a wedding present.

He hadn't seen her for ages. Perhaps the last time was that night he'd scared her. But, from time to time, she sent her 10-year-old sister, Klara. And the sick man grew very fond of the small child, calling her Mouse because she was so quick, and pretty, and fond of titbits. And it turned out that Mouse began to feel herself superior to him in certain ways. She sensed he might need a little mothering. So, one day, she said that he was a child of hers, and a very stupid and clumsy one at that. She brought him a flower, or an apple, each time… or her own fresh young mouth, which was what he liked best.

After a long search, Werner found the right wood for the work, and set up one of the Madonnas facing him as a model. It was a large, sumptuous one, and Mouse's eyes lit up, as she gazed open-mouthed at so many colours and such splendour.

All of a sudden, the child said 'You know, this isn't the Virgin Mary at all actually'. Werner, who wasn't making much headway with the work, looked up. Mouse held her little dimpled hand clamped to her mouth and wouldn't go on.

'How?' Werner asked.

'Because – I can't say why' she said, and there was something dark and hesitant about her reply.

'Come on, you little minx,' he said, 'who is it then?'

Mouse snuggled against him.

'Saint Agatha maybe?' the young man asked, fondling her hair.

'Oh! no...'

'Saint Anne?'

Mouse shook her head uneasily.

Werner recited the names of all the female saints he could think of. But the child dismissed each suggestion ever more firmly, and eventually, pouting with impatience, said 'It's not a saint at all, silly! It's a person.'

Werner smiled.

'Guess... go on guess... oh, but you'll never guess.' Mouse said miserably. It made Werner uncomfortable. He noticed a hint of contempt crossed her face.

She sat straight down, and said 'Anne-Marie.'

The sick man went extremely pale. His white hands shook a little. He fell back in his chair and there, beside the tall sumptuous Madonna, he seemed to see Anne-Marie's image growing within it. At first, the child looked surprised and upset to see how serious and silent Werner had become. But then, when he jumped up suddenly to seize his crutches and, in a strange, raised voice, ordered her to follow him, she felt alarmed.

And then she became acutely afraid. She kept wanting to ask him 'What's the matter with you?' But the words wouldn't come because anxiety had tightened her throat, and her heart was beating crazily. So she just followed the dull sound of the sick man's crutches all the way to the end of the attic. When they got there, before she had time to adjust her eyes to the dark, Werner dragged her by the arm and asked her roughly 'It's Anne-Marie again, isn't it?'

Mouse couldn't see a thing. His grip was hurting her; but on the brink of tears, she summoned up courage, and mumbled 'Yes.'

'And this one?' Now, with her eyes wide open, what she saw seemed similar to the Madonna he'd been carving downstairs: 'That too.'

She felt him pulling her again. He was begging her for an answer, but he was menacing her too with his breathless questions: 'And this one?'

'Yes' Mouse admitted hastily. Then gradually, out of the darkness, she began registering the presences of tall, beautiful Anne-Maries on all sides. And her fear subsided a little. With genuine admiration, she said 'Ah', adding as if to protect herself from yet more questioning, 'All of them, all of them.'

Then Werner let go her arm. Staggering to the corner, he collapsed, exhausted, into the chair. His crutches fell to the floor with a clatter. Mouse shot him fearful, guarded glances. He looked so sad. The girl turned quickly away towards the assembled figures, tiptoeing from one to the next to inspect them, sucking her finger – all of them were Anne-Maries in wood.

❦

Werner kept his door closed – except to the old woman who brought him lunch. In the evening, she came to clear up, but his food was almost uneaten. By the light of a single candle, the sick man carved tirelessly late into the night. He became feverish: his hands trembled and grew numb with the effort. Earlier, the candle had whistled, the flame had leapt, guttered, and gone out. The darkness weighed heavy on his tired eyes. His hand suffered awful cramps but wouldn't let go of the knife. It carved on regardless, moving blindly but briskly across the grain. There was something violent about it. And there was Werner, imagining the Virgin Mary, the object of his devotion, would guide his tool and give his obedient hand the strength to reach beyond his imagination and bring out of the darkness those features that encompass everything sacred and heavenly.

He didn't give up. In the first light of dawn, he was still at work in spite of his aching eyes. He lifted the wooden figure into the uncertain light. And there she still was: the same woman looking back at him. And it was still Anne-Marie, Anne-Marie who was to be married in a few days' time. In a surge of brute force, he smashed the figurine against the windowsill and its head snapped off, tracing a great arc across the half-lit room until it came to rest. Werner let go of the piece of wood and plunged his fingers into his hair until he felt his nails piercing his flesh like cold metal screws.

Outside, the summer sun was rising. Greyness was melting from the roofs, and the jubilant songs of countless birds rose from the garden next door. Bleary-eyed, Werner stared into the depths of a purple splendour. He was unable to kneel because of his paralysis, but his despairing soul was already on its knees, and he clasped his hands in the air and begged in his fever:

'O Holy Virgin, above and beyond all this you do exist, and are not Anne-Marie. It is not your wedding that will be celebrated in the coming days. It is you, and you alone, I wish to glorify. Ever since God took back the gift of my legs, I have sculpted your image. Yours, do you hear! I raise my sculpted prayers to you with these poor powerless hands of mine. Have I never pleased you? Holy Virgin, my poor works cannot convey your goodness. But grant that I may make just one, just one in your true likeness; or capture an aspect of your essence, as the spark of an ember may glow with the light of the sun. I am filled with gratitude towards you. May the carving I shall make radiate with the light of your light, and the love of your love. Let not this carving be like the others, for you shall not be like Anne-Marie who is to celebrate her wedding in the coming days.'

His voice was colourless, and his hands slipped to his knees in exhaustion. With his eyes closed, he listened to the echo of his prayer. He remained motionless as children do after a long night of raging fever.

But several minutes later, he suddenly came to, and grasped a new piece of wood, felt it, and began with unnatural haste to work at it. His eyes kept anxious watch over the developing work taking shape beneath his blade. He now felt a sacred, triumphal force in him, and the unction of his prayer promised sweet and secret hope. He sensed each cut was different from the hundreds and thousands he'd made before. He must now succeed with a work so new and chaste and unlike anything he'd ever carved, not all in one, but the one which would stand apart from all others. A great inner joy gave him strength, and he didn't feel his tired, aching fingers. After several hours, which seemed like minutes to him, he paused, placed the work on the windowsill, and gazed with a dreamy smile at the delicate features emerging from the fragrant wood. They seemed veiled. A tender face of grief, like that of a woman leaving, which you can't quite make out any more– perhaps she's already too far away, or one of your eyes is full of tears. Suddenly, Werner was reminded of his poor sick mother, whom he had hardly known because she went to her grave, with her hands clasped, so early in his life. And, while he continued mechanically with the sculpture, his emotions soared backwards to that maternal love, and the small pale flowers, that he had almost forgotten.

It seemed as though someone had come through a door, jolting the sick man out of his dream. Adjusting his focus, he started to peer into the furthest reaches of the room. Dusk was already spreading its shroud. There was no-one there. But when he took up his work again, he knew someone was sitting next to him, carving. He bent over the statue as if to protect it. But whoever was there still managed to reach it, tearing and twisting the delicate sorrowful lines into something more solid and earthly – and more like Anne-Marie. Werner froze in horror. He must make one last stand. His tool moved to and fro, sparkling, delirious and fleeting, following grooves already cut, throwing up showers of shavings. He had to beat his rival to it. But the rival carved pitilessly, brutally, coolly and cynically destroying each and every feature the breathless Werner had cut. Eventually, it seemed to the sick man that his relentless efforts had been overcome, and that the enemy prevailed. Furious desperation burned inside him. His right hand shook and attacked the wood with ever more savage and incoherent cuts. His eyes could no longer keep up with it. So he looked through the window, into the red face of evening, and cried out 'It's either you or me.' During which time, his right hand kept up its frantic work, as if not his own any more. And the sharp knife was no longer shaping the hard wood. He was carving his own bleeding hands. ❧ **RMR translated by AS**

Translator's note

I was amazed to find this story's not been published in English before. But, in his lifetime, Rainer Maria Rilke produced just two short-story collections: *Am Leben Hin* (1898) and *Geschichten vom Lieben Gott* (1900). Our story is from the former, and was read by Rilke to Lou Andreas-Salomé on Whit Sunday 1897, when he was 21.

How can a story like this be overlooked by translators? One answer is that the later *Letters to a Young Poet* and *Malte Laurids Brigge* outclassed his earlier work. But I also wonder whether his early stories were too daring for their day. Some ridicule social mores, others are sacrilegious and sexual, and some show early signs of the surreal. Their full-blooded young author sits awkwardly with the more ascetic and mystical Rilke of the general consensus. In German, of course, the stories have been obtainable since they first appeared. French readers have had them since 1993, when La Pléiade published the complete prose works in one volume.

I fell for this story for its psychological rawness, its focus on the uncontrollable in the creative process, its recognition of the entanglements of sexuality and religion, and their devastating effect on a vulnerable psyche. It is likely that Rilke's obsession with Lou, whom he'd met only weeks before, provided the model for Werner's crisis in the story, brought on by Anne-Marie and the Madonnas he's made, and the way they all merge in his desire. ❦ AS

Poems

In the Shrewsbury Wimpy

Someone's television new-bolted
to a high corner, pouring out loud,
light dance videos; tiny daughter-
of-franchisee glued to it, printing

potato-print replicas of each move
with the brief length of herself,
limby, everywhere, bouncing giddy
singalong off the formica; scoliotic

teacup stacks; grandfatherly waiters
laughing together, rising to ferry
donuts with outmoded cream hairdos,
ouroboric hot dogs, heavy plates, heavy

serviettes, cutlery – cutlery! Outside,
moss, rampant on the dead
way we live. It doesn't know
the rock it hugs is *ailing*

burger chain brick, thinks
it's *mountain*; thrusts its hot orange
spears into the clouds' low belly –
for we are alive! All of us!

Alive on the top of the mountain!   ❦ JN

Horologist

Engineer of clocks and watches

To be his apprentice
would mean relinquishing
my future. Brightness
was his shop's defining
feature then, that same
gleam articulated
by steel bezels or crystal-
cracked circles of glass.
Too young to own time
or know where it was
headed I am his afterimage
as the second-hand
is to the first. Watching
him take the watch apart
in wiry glasses so like
an undertaker's I felt time
not ceasing but looping
his tweezers slipping
the dead's rubies
into glistening innards.

❧ EY

Fully dedicated to the craft

striking consonance.

Shadowing to learn his skill

*The face of a clock, circular.
Time stops for a dead watch*

*I wonder if jewellery
is donated for repurposing
in this way?... Adds sentiment
to a watch.*

Fishkeeping

We don't sell rasbora here, I told the personification of death. His face seemed gaunt in the store's faux moonlight. The next morning, I was pumping the goldfish bags with oxygen when I got a call informing me a curse would soon befall a yet-to-be-born relative. Ignore it, said my boss. I hung up and fastened the knot. Then I visited my grandfather in the ward, though his face no longer recognised me. Did anyone bring winter melon soup? I looked up and spotted, in his intravenous bag, a red rasbora.

❧ EY

[handwritten annotations:]

> Small freshwater fish from SE

Like the rela? in hospital

Death's face reappearing in relative?

> Great consonance Red = evil, dangerous col A warning? Contradicts the opening line say they don't sell yet one appear elsewhere.

That Year

That year she moved into a microwave
was the year of caricature.

Small, hot place?

Inside the minibus radio's electric snow
was the fifth album of a one-hit wonder.

Great description of feedback/crackle

Dinner was lunch divided in tupperware
resuscitated with invisible rays.

Bulk/batch cooking, re-heating in a microwave

Was there an evolutionary purpose to roaches?
She thought the salted fish might know.

Rain, external and sudden,
towing slogans, post-its, cursory promises

into drains sworn to the city's declension.
The pork was minced and sweet

For rain (noun) to "tow" (verb), it must be strong. Tsunami? Storm?

decline/deterioration

and glass is just the means
through which the world dissolves the world.

❦ EY

Windows to seperate?
Microwave glass containing the heat?

Canopy

Anchored in shallow stony ditches
two cottonwoods built their circular staircases
80 feet high, around columns
of absolute nerve. In their shade
we'd make our fire to picnic
on the road allowance, which seems so strange
though at the time it was hardly a road
at all, no gas well trucks or corporate farms,
and it made us feel lucky and far away,
so few trees around, so little rain.
We learned the word 'canopy,' it was like
a miracle, owlets peering
through their nursery window to where we sat
on the graded dirt, and the smoke
from our hot dog fire rose straight up.
It was the same, Dad said,
when he was a child, owlets
in their canopy beds, time eddying
deep in the shelter of the cottonwoods
where demands of the yard and fields
couldn't enter, as though by a spell
we didn't cast but that welcomed us.
The heavy equipment passes
beneath them more often now,
edges of the widened road approach

Handwritten annotations:
- Top treeline cover
- Deep roots
- branches?
- Rise of industry and capitalism taking over rural spots
- A place to rest, away from the hard work the farm

yet they are there still, in excess
of their average lifespan
and function. In spring
they champagne the air with cotton.

Very long-lived trees

❦ KS

Blossom

great use as a verb

Next Life

great assonance

Someone desiring the blue of the sky was sold this earthly
mis-tint, a wall colour that even in daylight feels
threadbare, solitary, a little irritable, possibly lead-based,

Clues of elderly relative's house

a blue that suits a crucifix in pride of place
above the TV on its rolling collapsible metal stand.
It's getting to be about that time to switch the lamps on.

When she died, not much could be passed down. What she owned
worn through the core of its function, in rags
or with the true nature of its construction exposed.

Beloved objects were of no worth
absent of her regard. And it was more than that, as though
the spirit of her belongings, any remnants of utility and charm,

had chosen to accompany her into the next life. The world
used her right up, along with the little she'd been given.
But everything she'd been given she found a use for.   ❦ KS

A nice idea

Grateful; utilised

Cadmium Lemon

Not hot
like fickle summer,
more like sun smudged
under a thumb, mocked
by toxic shadows, belch
of smoke, endless
driving rain.

It's a sour kiss
on sallow skin, a stench
of sulphur in the air,
jaundiced slide to distance
you didn't notice until
you were on the other side.

It's the yell-
          ow of hazard,
of hornet, a fake gold locket,
a bottle blonde. It warms you
with false promise, even as
you try to catch its
failing light.   ❦ TY

handwritten annotations:

Cd = carcinogenic element. Causes lung/prostate cancer

Yellow =
☺ Joy, Happiness, optimism
☹ Jealousy, cowardice, caution

Muggy, weak, blurry

→ pollution

→ acid rain ?

→ Unhealthy, pale. Also sounds like "yellow".

→ Death?

"yell" → shout
"ow" → pain

• Breaking the word "Yellow" to reframe each syllable as different words

Sibling

Ask me about the ubiquitous
little sister.

She rubs sandwich meat between her hands
and begins her righteous parade

leading the street's dogs
on a scurrilous walk:

three times already she's
blamed me to shame me.

When she reaches my porch,
she shines like a lighthouse

summoning all believers.
If she feels any qualm,

she turns to the dogs:
Look, she says, as they lick

her chickened hands,
see how they love me.   ❧ CE

Song of the West Pier

And when your face falls off,
    keep stumbling. When you're caked
with shit and the smashed train
    of your torso gives way, totter forth.

So what if all your pretty starlings left
    and you're a sieve for the wind,
a rigid flock of nothings?
    When your iron legs are trapped,

stagger forward in your head, fragmenting
    with every step but closer already
to your goal by reeling,
    like the pummelled moon, on and on –

❦ JMC

Age of Retirement

The news is delivered in neon yellow pulsations. I am aware of the latest wars, famines, movies, and business stories.

It seems the wellness proprietor has become disconsolate. Customers' expectations are not what they used to be.

You are in the garden, tending the seedlings like a grudge. Greenhouses were seen as obscenely progressive once.

Now everything is possible and very little is pleasant. Across the street, a little girl in a knitted hat waves hello.

I lift my fingers automatically. She will learn soon enough. I anticipate her disappointment on finding the park closed.

❦ DF

The Music of the Spheres

i.m. Michael Longley

The pre-Socratics I imagine
as a kind of jazz band:
Anaximander laying down
perpetual motion on the pan flute,
Protagoras with the measure
of all things on lyre, Thales
and Heraclitus trading solos
like ice and fire. The way
Anaxagoras preaches it, the soul
is like a bucket of water forever
catching fire and putting
its own flames out. There is one
story and one story only, drums
Parmenides on tympanon,
but love o love and strife,
it's warring contraries
make life, Empedocles croons.
Too busy to pick up a kithara,
Pythagoras has visions
of heavenly harmonies
he's calling the music of
the spheres, as emitted
by the moon, sun and stars,
their chosen key of silence

reminding me that a good tune
can never be played the same way...
never, Zeno leans in
to correct me in advance,
never be played the same way once.   🐝 DW

Cuthbert

'whose initial, / lost in Lindisfarne plaited lines'
Basil Bunting

I, gratitude of tucked nest
by God's cliff and cranny,
doing my little dance, doing
they will call by my name.
of habit not feather,
I, mattress of rock and turf in
I, weightiness of
I, measured in wood
of His tree. I, bride of blood
letter of the cloudless text.
replica, decoy, remembrance.
The difficulty of putting
I, not so sure of my own
whetstone, tracing in skerry
I, this wave and this wave
in a different day. I, lost,

sheltered in shit stench
pilfering the crags of trash cans,
my little dance to the birds
I, word-hoard man and man
neighbour to Faith alone.
Canny Beds Massive Savings!
wind upon land upon wind.
of Rood, wedded by rings
and will. I, winding
I, mappa mundi fridge magnet:
I, sprayed with unfound.
faces to names!
now, at home on this grey
braille of the Word.
coming up for air
migrating into marble. ❧JW

[handwritten annotations:]
1st Person : Cuddy)
Modern Age?
Lindisfarne gift shop?
READING DIRECTION → ↓ × ✓
Small rocky island
Lost to history only memorials?
why the fragmented split? to look biblical?

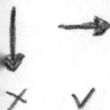

In the Temple in the Mountain South of the Western Gate

We were lost on the way to the temple.

But this was not a big problem, the first thirty minutes of parking were free.

The faces of the apotropaic figures on the gates were mostly worn away, leaving only glaring open eyes. This made them more effective.

On the stairs to the highest building, a desiccated, flattened worm being carried off by large black ants.

This meant something, though I'm afraid of making pronouncements. It was not profound.

There were signs asking visitors to please close the doors to the shrines so cats wouldn't get in, but to our disappointment there were no cats in sight.

And what if a cat should desire to see the Buddha?

Don't all creatures deserve to bow 108 times?

When we opened the door, next to the gleaming Bodhisattva, a portrait of the murdered dictator and his murdered wife.

I cannot say what it means.

The windchime in the shape of an eyeless fish, the cawing of unseen crows.

Looming above all, a rocky peak whose silhouette is in many famous paintings.

Below us all, a magpie patiently hopping up the meaningless steps.

❧ **SHB**

Her Wellness Journey

sweat me no reveries. insomnia's obstinate séance.
the pressure to suffer correctly. the world is xerox
through cognitive fog. clairvoyeurism. watching.
a ghost in our house. *ideation* is not an *idea*. well,
maybe. have set my jaw against the day. slick with
conspiracy, the *bitches*. they do not know: *by any
means necessary, by any means available*. this is
my body, cannot contain its decline. these pearly,
palisaded cells. the wiry strife of it. the stripped
wire of it. *my body, politely saucerised. bitches.*
the *winners*. their rosy agenda is juice. tossing
the mane of monologue. the mane of miracle. i
am inside. fulminate humbug. the curtains are
drawn against broadcast. tight. in the night-
sweat redolent bed, evict myself from pity. no,
i will *not go gentle* into this segue of numinous
dread. but fuck that commonly decent pout.
and fuck that green, hubristic egg.   🌱 FL

Poetry of the 'Nineties

Henry Newbolt led the cheers for God
and England. Rudyard Kipling's ballads crash-
bang-walloped like a brass band. WE Henley
saw the future in a novel-reading barmaid.
Alice Meynell chose Rome. Lord Alfred Douglas
was famous for other things. Lionel Johnson
drank. John Todhunter struck the Celtic note.
Theodore Wratislaw cultivated hothouse flowers.
Richard Le Gallienne called streetlights 'lamps of sin'.
Katharine Harris Bradley and Edith Emma Cooper
were Michael Field. Francis Thompson followed
De Quincey into opium and squalor. John Barlas
took a blow to the head and died confined.
Ah socialism, but also sweet spring blossom,
Dollie Radford told Marx. The absent
Amy Levy's omnibus terminated
in 1889. Alfred Austin [*muffled laughter*].
Pound would sweep up Victor Plarr for *Mauberley*.
When Yeats met Verlaine, they communicated
in a form of dumbshow. The ballads AE
Housman struck up after a glass of ale
had a faintly murderous edge. Oscar Wilde
was *not* carrying a copy of *The Yellow
Book* when arrested at the Cadogan Hotel.
Ernest Dowson coined the word 'soccer'.

Amid the swirling ectoplasm at the séance
Olive Custance felt a ghostly hand on her thigh.
Versified by Yeats, Walter Pater
entertained dreams of vague Greek boys
while his sisters fried his sausages. What
the bloody hell do you want, asked Swinburne
naked, answering the door to George Moore.
Growing overstimulated, Arthur
Symons collapsed and survived himself
by decades. As John Davidson's body
washed out of Penzance the far lights
of Scotland would have lain hard to starboard.   ❦ DW

Salt Solution

After three hours of distilled blue, the aquarium will have me
    weeping. The octopi will have me sob
as they squish themselves beyond each plastic shipwreck.
My line of sight may motion, then, a cos or a tan or a sine
  wave. Mustard, cross-gartering a hotdog. I will cry
    like I do when I'm hungry and forced to make some policy
shift seem sexy to my colleagues. Unprompted, I will have
    snotted on my cufflinks and the motive will then fast be-
come the flustering itself.

                    Fluid chokes the pyrex.

                        Salt zig-
    zags down the contours of an eye. Yet I am as empty as an
octopus: its weight pressed upon the pane, now, the suckers
    taking nothing from the glass, or the tourists, or the rock-
face of my cheekbone. Perhaps I have no stake in its splayed
  beak, or lack a second heart from which I reach out to my own.

                                    ❦ JBR

In That We Know Quicksand
Likes a Wriggler

There are two approaches when entering a room. You might scurry, head like a malady, ducked snug as you pace down an aisle. The talk has started and you

are made more visible in apology. You must learn that the best food is not fortified but natural, in that everything now swills in microplastic caramel.

Enter each alternate room as boldly as a stick insect in motion. Stand before the crowd and wiggle your opposable thumbs. They're a testament to youth.

This is the 68th stage of grief, the one in which I bring an inventory: a tassel, a nipple, a knife (for our gunfights), a bucket, spade and premade sandcastle.

I look forward to the next one: my long wink to the camera, through which
you ascertain that I am light, despite the last time that my grief was weighed.

The wind keeps us alert at the seaside. We stand to attention, in that we know
how to posture as a mermaid might in orchestrated sand. It's all that we can bear

to hold. This fistful of flat pebbles. This once. To enter the division that we know
to be a coastline. Respond to each sinking. Turn, to see if they are watching, again.

❦ JBR

Screamin' Grey Parrot

[handwritten annotation: The poet's use of metaphor ↑]

The language of animals is sensible. Mine is not. This is my latest ode to the imagination. Something in me is wounded meaning I can't really enjoy it, place no stock in it. Pre-undermined and absent any consolation. That's my gift for the altar. I know the path I'm on. Animals get me, even if I don't. The Book of Kells has feet and legs of beasts that don't go anywhere, consistent squiggles for a human face: 'heraldic', which is how we might interpret anything. Some animals find me too eager to please. Once I met a grey parrot in a tall black cage. I liked the grey parrot at once – he was beautiful, like a theatre critic from the 1920s. The moment I entered the room he looked directly at me and started screaming – a constant, uninterrupted scream louder than a burglar alarm. I spoke in a soothing voice, made my movements gentle and uncertain, but the more I tried to remonstrate the louder the grey parrot screamed and screamed until I had to make my excuses to the host – inaudible beneath the parrot's scream – and leave the dinner party altogether. A grey parrot can live for up to sixty years, so that was pretty much the end of that love story / business venture.

It's okay if you have business ventures. I don't judge and I trust your money. Carrington was very good at making domestic rituals horrifying, dim grey halation, sacrificial dinners with odd implements. Untitled lithograph entitled 'Secret Intelligence'. I love you so much it's structural. I love your every second thought.

Vibrating constantly, angels expend 90% of their energy on the sheer effort required to be visible to us for a fraction of a second. Sacred geometry shaken to pieces. An absence in the shape of a country in the sea. The chores of reenchantment. Where will you anchor your life?

❦ LK

Turbo

In the fifty-fifty eventuality
that I'm gone before you
you can clip the caps off all my lipsticks
the half-used and the nearly
-thered carefully crescented to
the average of both my lips I recommend
NARS *Turbo* for this – something
about the formula clings so cleanly
to the uptake of me of me of you   ❦ **AB**

The day
after, in shock
but warm, at the barber's
we discuss how this thing could have
happened.

We are
safe, still, together,
five tattooed men and I
listening to Nigel talking
softly

about
his time training
to be a barber by
shaving a balloon. He found it
stressful.

🥀 AK

The Hierophant

True enough, but it can only be stated so many times
    before it starts losing its lustre. And so it was
        in the early days the villagers used to set it to music
to extend its shelf-life, the way the old fishmonger
    always packed his catch in salt, or in ice chipped off
the forehead of the mountain. This was before the glacier
    had withdrawn completely, leaving in its wake an abundance
        of tiny beautiful meltwater lakes, most of which burst

through their banks in time, flooding the village
    and surrounding farmland. A few have kept intact,
        teeming with what appear to be trout, but if you look
through the water's still surface, right knee bent
    in thick tufts of grass, you can begin to make out
all the tiny telltale differences. Where the fish came from
    remains a mystery, and you will devote your life
        to solving it, contending with the herons and kingfishers

said to feed here in season. Maybe one day a black bear
    takes you by surprise! Rearing on its haunches,
        majestic even in its hunger, it's hard not to see why
our ancestors worshipped them. But as the visits
    grow commonplace, the bear becomes a nuisance.
If you do take on an assistant, it's only in the hope
    that a little youthful enthusiasm might liven things up
        here in the final stretch, and not in answer to any need

related to the research, which you already completed
    years ago, remember – amid the worst of the wildfires.
        It's mostly just a matter of typing things up at this point,
finishing touches. Someone to share in the glory –
    to remember how it once was. You can't offer very much
in terms of compensation, just a small weekly stipend,
    room and board. There's a studio apartment in the barn
        out back. After tidying up, sit in sunlight on the far corner

of its freshly made bed, in the pink-copper-red of the glow
    stampeding through the window. The contentment
        you felt impending won't come, or it came and went
unnoticed. Still, there's quiet, long cold quiet and the sense that
    everything that will ever be asked of you
has been asked. The villagers gathered in the hall have
    all been waiting for you to appear. But before you can clear
        your throat to speak, the light evaporates in applause.

        ❦ TD

Girls Without Clothes

1.

Always the fact of what is said: undress
Show your   take off   lie there
Lay your   open your   let me see
Part your   touch my   did you see?
Always the room with the flat
Surface   you stand like a tree   always
Lie like a tree   felled   always
Branches stiffly outstretched

Soil between your fingers   fingers in your mouth
Couldn't save the apples.

2.

Always a season   for which
There is nothing   it undresses her
Undresses anything that stands in its wind
And there is no resisting
Your apples your skin your husk   gone
Your hair your nipples your eyes   (did you see?)
(she lay there like a log) (why so wooden?)
(part) (open) (show me your pears your plums)

Always a room where everything happens.
Always something that can be stripped.

3.

It is always spring and we stood apart
Arms apart and legs and folds open in the bark
And anyone who wanted could peer into
The very heartwood, to where the flesh was still
Moist   even appearing vaporous.
In such weather the living grows unsheathed
Headless, letting its hair loose into the wind
Allowing itself to be examined and demonstrated, and

Fingers inserted to the point where the heart becomes wood.
It is always spring and the rooms are filled with damp forest.

4.

It is always autumn   everything stripped   everything split
Flung open   lying in an ugly heap
Outer clothes   underclothes outer branches   undergrowth
White roots   struggling free of the earth
Ear lobes   head aches
The apples of the eye   the limbs of the body
Lips of the head, the body's lips, tongue of the mouth and the body
Digits of hand and foot, someone else's fingers

Between the fingers and the toes, there, there's a
Knot   a knotted bundle   tie it up a keepsake don't look.

5.

It is always summer and the girl without clothes
Is always fifteen, sometimes more, sometimes less
Fifteen is the number of filthy stains
Tiles you slide in the game of fifteen
With the girl without clothes: every touch
Leaves a stain   a tiny bruise under the skin
After a while you begin to wear them loose
Like the pelt of a dead creature   an ermine cloak

You wear yourself like a dead ermine
Windfalls fingers always bruised apples ankles

6.

Always winter, chilly without clothes, fingers
Lift to the mouth   from the mouth steam lifts
Into the sky   someone's staircase and always
Up and down   these or others rise
Paying no attention to the girls without clothes
So cold those girls   frozen to the spot always
Winter, the adam's apple of the watcher
(open show take)   moves back and forth

Heart carries the water up and down the stairs
Waters the roots to your heart's delight, woodman.

7.

Always fifteen   sometimes more   sometimes much more
Always much less, like a child at nursery school
Told to take down its pants   and all the round eyes
Rolling to follow   the naked sun   where
Always one and the same   rising   rising.
Always fingers, apples   skilled at prizing apart
And eating   parting and taking   taking a
Part   undressing and tasting   opening and entering   leaving

And it rises, rises over
The little rounded mound of Venus.

8.

There is always a hunter   who desires to know
Always a viewer   who desires to view
While his apples swell in their sockets
Look   little ermine   running away up
The body of the hunter   who desires to hold
And higher up the tree   the stiff tree
Attempts no escape   nor resists   nor feels shame.
These lips closed (open)   these mouths open

(part and give) the little beast struggling to its freedom
While her naked body occupies your attention.

9.

There is always pornography   always
Veiled   in pale   cellophane
As if to say to you   you are my first
He/she always says to her   take it all off
Part the pages   show me what you've got
Always there the girls without clothes.
Their fingers ready to bloom, their buds
Ready to put out leaves   boles

Dark   fair   body-coloured   lit with bodily light
If you order them to   they will look at you.

10.

There is almost always clothes on the
Girls without clothes   it makes them more
Undressed   wrap a scarf around the tree
Or a blanket, and the bare wood of the tree
(The naked body of the body) is a place
Of shame. Almost always
They wear warm bloomers, worn shoes
Stockings wrinkled around the ankles

They are marked by a bra strap   a bruise   a cross
What you will want   to remove

11.

Always girls without clothes.
Always something to eat them up.
Always something uneaten, left over.
Always something that will never be again.
Will never go out onto the boardwalk
Twisting an ancient lemon-coloured parasol
Like the rolling wheel of the sun
A woman of the street, someone else's sex worker.

Here, the only photograph of her
Offering up the round sun of her bottom.

12.

Girls without clothes always
Say the same thing: they say yes   they say yes
For that is the only word in their tongue
Which has been translated into others.
In sealed mouths yes puts out shoots   grows
Entangles another's tongue invades another's mouth
And always woodman hunter fisherman
Wakes one day with a hook in his tongue

Hooked tongue lays prone in the darkness
Girl without clothes stands silently.

13.

Soldiers always standing at their post   trees
Always standing their ground   corpses lying always
In the earth and on it, and always impossible
To know whose leg is   whose
Lovers, wound into each other
And shining through their embraces their blankets
Their bellies, like luminescent fish,
The oranges they broke in two to eat.

In your head there is always a closed room
And in it stands the girl without clothes.

14.

Are you always this wooden?
I bet you must be a passionate girl?
You just a cold woman?
Have you ever kissed anyone?
Do you like this? Shall I show you how?
Show me the dark down   the belly button
Ear lobes   nipples   slippers   beads   vertebrae
Apples of the eyes   closed   dry

Bought from the gypsies so she could undress with pride
Red satin lace panties

15.

We were fifteen   and it was always the way.
At fifteen
Curiosity and shame suffuse the body
Expanding like a balloon. Mother said to cure
Hiccups fill your mouth with air   hold it as long as you can.
Curiosity and shame made me silent
As if I held water in my mouth. Then and always
My legs like water   when I stand without clothes

You enter parting the water with your hands.
It is me   it is me   pocket of air

🍂 **MS translated by SD**

What would

you put here?

Re-Reading

❦ DS

'*What does a man do with his silence?*'

'Come to listen to this freak'

For the uninitiated, RS Thomas was born in 1913 in Cardiff, and raised in Holyhead in Anglesey. For the rest of his life he would – self-confessedly – wrestle with the wound of his anglicised up-bringing, which he felt had denied him the Welsh language and divided him from what ought to have been a stabilising national identity. This search for an 'authentic' Welsh belonging would follow a trajectory ever westward into the hills: From Manafon in Montgomeryshire – where Thomas became rector in 1942, and where he began learning Welsh – to Cardiganshire in 1954, and on to the remote Welsh-speaking parish of Aberdaron at the tip of the Llyn peninsula.

Throughout his life Thomas published over 30 books and was the recipient of numerous awards, including the Queen's Gold Medal for poetry. In 1996 he was nominated for the Nobel Prize in Literature (but pipped to the post by Wisława Szymborska).

Despite these honours, his critical reputation has continued to sine-wave, with English critics in particular striving alternately to assimilate him or to distance him from their conception of the national canon. Even the poet's death in 2000 did little to stabilise these unwieldy oscillations, at the heart of which – enigmatic and implacable – stood the ambivalent and fractalised figure of Thomas himself, a tree 'Without roots, but with many branches.'

Ambivalence attended Thomas's reception within English literary culture. Ambivalence was the hallmark of the man. But more than this, ambivalence is a theme and a mode in his work: a conscious and highly dynamic poetic strategy emerging from a radical anti-materialist ethics, and from his colonial situation. I think so anyway. I'm not a Thomas (or any other kind) of scholar. What I am is a fellow poet-practitioner, and a recent but zealous convert; as a queer ex-crusty, I hadn't expected to have my head turned by this most austere of Anglican rectors.

I met RS Thomas for the first time, not in poetry, but in his *Selected Prose* (1986). I met him in a vivid description of his life as rector at St Michael's church in Manafon, near Welshpool. Thomas was rector there from 1942 to 1954, during which time he published three collections of poetry: *The Stones of the Field* (1946), *An Acre of Land* (1952) and *The Minister* (1953). During this period he also began to study Welsh with a neighbouring clergyman. As I read, I was struck by a passage in which Thomas makes his first faltering efforts to express himself publicly in Welsh. He is addressing his Welsh-speaking neighbour's chapel. He sets the scene:

> I remember the evening: the chapel with its oil lamps, the wind blowing outside, and about twenty local farm-

ers and their wives, come to listen to this freak – an Eng-
lishman who had learnt Welsh.

It was the phrase 'this freak' that shocked me into retuned at-
tention, a pejorative then followed by Thomas's characterisation
of himself as 'an Englishman'. Thomas was born in Cardiff to
Welsh parents. He was anglicised, but he *was* Welsh. One of the
few things I knew about Thomas at the time of reading those
words is that he was Welsh. The Welshness of RS Thomas is, in
fact, routinely – interminably – emphasised wherever his name
is mentioned. Not *just* Welsh, mind, but a *passionate* advocate
for Welsh language and culture (often misidentified as a rabid
and backward-looking nationalism). So, this description is jar-
ring. With it, Thomas distils an absolute sense of estrangement,
slanting the conventions of autobiography, and viewing himself
through the eyes of the congregation: an isolated community in
the midst of which he is doubly isolated. I was powerfully arrest-
ed by the loneliness of that image: a 'freak', after all, is a spectacle,
and nowhere are you more alone than as the subject of the stare.
　This feeling is not unknown to me, as an Anglophone person
of Irish Traveller heritage: to be an outsider within one's native
culture; to wrestle with a 'foreign' language that ought to be your
mother tongue. I joke that I have only *one* language, and that it
isn't my own. Describing his move to Manafon, Thomas speaks
of himself disparagingly as a 'proper little bourgeois, brought up
delicately, with the mark of the church and the library on me'.
The mark, in other words, of English habits, customs, culture –
and language. *This* is the passage that sent me searching out the
poetry of RS Thomas. Was *he* on a kindred quest to unmake the
pain and the problem of English with English? To find, within

the precincts of poetry, a way of forcing that unhomely home to make room for him?

I began at the beginning. *The Stones of the Field* (1946) opens with 'Out of the Hills', a kind of mythopoetic inverse pilgrimage that introduces not only a looming archetype or antagonist in Thomas's work – that of the Welsh Hill Peasant – but also the preoccupations – some might say *obsessions* – that would come to distinguish and dominate his writing: the special spiritual character of the Welsh hill country and its people, the enigmatic silence of a distant God, the destruction of Welsh land, language and tradition by wanton materialism. It's a bold opening salvo. And it has this compellingly strange symmetry: while Thomas's unnamed peasant is 'ambling' out of the hills towards the reader, Thomas himself is striding *into* them. Thomas came to the rectory at Manafon from the Flintshire border country of Hanmer, his nerves shredded by the nightly war-time terror he experienced there, as German planes flew overhead on their way to 'drop their evil load on helpless women and children' in Merseyside. In his autobiography *Neb* – or, in its English translation, *Nobody* (1985) – Thomas writes that 'he so longed for the hills in the distance [...] that he decided to learn Welsh, in order to come back to Wales.' This 'coming back', the idea of a return that is both territorial and psychic, that takes place with and through language, of a return – moreover – that can never be completed, is a significant feature of the poem, and a persistent presence in Thomas's work.

Yet the hills to which Thomas returns, and from which the figure in the poem emerges, are not places of uncomplicated ease or psychological safety. This is the *land*, not the *landscape*; its mode of existence is pitiless, indifferent. Its inhabitants are not quaint rustics, they are perverse survivalists, as uncouth and as obdurate as the bedrock from which they are forged. In the first four lines alone, the poem's antagonist arrives:

> Dreams clustering thick on his sallow skull,
> Dark as curls, he comes, ambling with his cattle
> From the starved pastures. He has shaken from off his
>   shoulders
> The weight of the sky, and the lash of the wind's sharpness

Yes, we are in a space of dreaming, a place of mythopoetic enchantment, but there's nothing abstract or inconsequential about what is taking place here; this is an enchantment that leaves a somatic imprint on and in the body: the *weight* of the sky, the *sharpness* of the wind, driving all before it like a whip drives cattle. There is a heaviness to the diction too, those long, irregular lines – and just listen to that kink in 'shaken from off', as if it were designed to trip the (English) reader – strung together by knots of sound: *sallow, ambling, cattle, pastures, lash*, giving the poem a swinging sonic gait, half swagger and half stumble. And the *verbs!* Just look at how they place the subject at the centre of a constant tactile happening. These 'dreams' are not peaceful, they are a space of vivid sensation and restless motion: *clustering, ambling, shaken, starved.*

And if Thomas's peasant dreams, 'the legendary town' toward which he is headed dreams too, 'Dreams of his coming' while 'under the half-closed lids / Of the indolent shops sleep dawdles'. A trick is being played here, a trap is being set to spring. The peasant *thinks* he is dreaming of the town, but the town has set a snare for him, exerting its baleful, patient pull like something alive and incalculably cunning. As he is drawn towards it 'The shadow of the mountain dwindles' and 'his scaly eye / Sloughs its cold care and glitters.' Which – apart from anything else – is an exhilarating bit of phrase-making that Thomas uses to signal his subject's descent into a modern material world of drunkenness and fevered dissipation. A 'chorus of coins sings in his tattered pockets', as we follow him into the streets of his 'swift undoing', and the 'sudden disintegration / Of his soul's hardness'. This is a verdict remarkable in its severity, but entirely consonant with Thomas's views on modernity (more of those anon) and the way in which he understood the spiritual stakes involved in leaving those hills.

There is hope (of a sort) for Thomas's antagonist. In the last four lines of the poem we are told to wait for him, that:

At midnight he will return,
Threading the tunnel that contains the dawn
Of all his fears. Be then his fingerpost
Homeward. The earth is patient; he is not lost.

There *is* a certain tenderness to this conclusion – with its overtones of Christly resurrection – which extends the promise of restitution and spiritual recovery. Yet I found myself disquieted by Thomas's line breaks: 'Threading the tunnel that contains the dawn' is markedly different to 'Threading the tunnel that contains the dawn / Of all his fears', this last catching us – the reader – off-guard, as we might imagine the subject is caught, experiencing the instinctive chill that sends him hurrying back through the darkness into the hills. I wonder too about that gap between 'fingerpost' and 'Homeward', that long unsettled moment before our peasant finds his path. Thomas creates, on one level, an allegory in which he pits the sly, corrupting patience of Mammon against the elemental impassivity of God in a contest for the soul of man. Yet, on another level, Thomas's wayward herder is *absolutely* real; his is an *inner* struggle between Welsh rural rootedness (and the spiritual authenticity this represents), and the seductions of modernity and mechanisation. Neither of these opposing forces seem to use him gently. 'The earth is patient' contains, I think, a premonition of the grave.

And *that* was my entry into the poetry of RS Thomas. Promised that his peasant would return, I sought him out. I did not have to look too far. He appears numerous times in *The Stones of the Field*, as 'A Labourer' whose skin 'the winds have stretched' on the 'bare racks of bone', and crystallising most famously and most forcibly as Iago Prytherch, who appears by name for the first time in 'A Peasant', where he is described as – amongst other, less value-neutral judgements – 'an ordinary man of the bald Welsh hills'. Prytherch is an avatar Thomas would return to time and again, figuring him in a variety of ways throughout his career. In *The Stones of the Field* and in *An Acre of Land*, Prytherch seems to represent an amalgam of the labourers, herdsmen and hill farmers who arrested and – in Thomas's own words – 'compelled' the poet's gaze. Towards 1955 and the publication of *Song at the Year's Turning* – Thomas's first collection of poems from an English publisher – Prytherch was certainly in the process of becoming something far stranger and more substantial: a persistent enigma, an alter ego, a (mostly) silent interlocutor, an aspect of the poet's own troubled conscience and consciousness.

Even from the beginning Thomas's representation of this 'ordinary man' is complex and ambivalent, full of frustrated admiration and fascinated revulsion. The portrait he paints is not, by any means, kindly. In 'A Peasant' he declares that "There is something frightening in the vacancy of his mind. / His clothes, sour with years of sweat / And animal contact, shock the refined'. Not nice. Here speaks Thomas the snob, the 'refined', the self-confessed 'proper little bourgeois', the 'Englishman', turning a colonially conditioned eye on the native inhabitants of his adopted hill country. And yet, in the last six lines, a more nuanced picture emerges:

> Yet this is your prototype, who season by season
> Against siege of rain and the wind's attrition,
> Preserves his stock, an impregnable fortress
> Not to be stormed even in death's confusion.
> Remember him, then, for he, too, is a winner of wars,
> Enduring like a tree under the curious stars.

It's bombastic, sure, but it's also deeply impressive. And as M Wynn Thomas (not relation) has noted, it's hard not to read that final couplet in the context of Thomas's retreat to Manafon from Hanmer; both his animal fear and his moral repulsion in the face of the war and its mechanised murder. In *The Echoes Return Slow* (1988), a memoir written in alternate passages of poetry and prose, Thomas writes of the gnawing doubts that beset him during this period:

> Yes, action has its compensations. What does one do when one does not believe in action, or in certain kinds of action? Are the brave lacking in imagination? Are the imaginative not brave, or do they find it more difficult to

be brave? What does a man do with his silence, his alone-
ness, but suffer the sapping of unanswerable questions?

Prytherch, who offers a model for an existence proof against
such questions, allows Thomas to articulate and confront both
his horror of war, and – paradoxically – his sneaking disgust at
his own cowardice in the face of war, his envy of 'men of action'.
It is striking that Prytherch too is a 'winner of wars', not modern
technological warfare, with its doomed hubristic will to power
(and concomitant jingoism), but something akin to survival it-
self. The lesson of Prytherch is that bravery may not, after all,
reside in the conquest of heroes, but in the endurance of stoics.

In *RS Thomas: Serial Obsessive* (2013) M Wynn Thomas finds
a useful comparison between 'A Peasant' and 'Homo Sapiens
1941'. The only poem in *Stones of the Field* to deal explicitly with
war, 'Homo Sapiens' treats of the flight (and fall) of a modern
aviator, intoxicated by his own mad daring. It contains some
thrillingly strange runs of language, beginning: 'Murmuration of
engines in the cold caves of air' and ending with 'But loud as a
drum in his ear the hot blood sings, / And a frenzy of solitude
mantles him like a god'. Of this singular poem M Wynn Thom-
as writes: 'it is with reference to "Homo Sapiens 1941" that RS
Thomas's early farmer poems acquire a pointed "period" meaning
that immediately politicises them. To put it simply, Prytherch is
the elemental opposite of "Homo Sapiens 1941" – earth-bound
where the latter is air-borne, doggedly ancient where the latter
is dangerously modern'. In other words, Prytherch is a figure
around whom Thomas constellates various forms of refusal: cer-
tainly of war, and of the spurious seductions of the machine age.
But *also* – and to me this is just as significant – of Enlightenment

ideas around mastery over nature.

When 'Homo Sapiens 1941' was reprinted in *Song at the Year's Turning* in 1955, Thomas placed it beside 'A Labourer'. The remorseless, motiveless action of the winds is implicated in the fate of both airman and peasant: 'legions of winds' 'ambush' the former, and ultimately conspire at his destruction; wind stretches taut the skin of the labourer who is shaped and honed by the elements, *not* annihilated by them. Weathering, for Thomas, means both wearing away and long outlasting. For him, the natural world is not something to challenge, to master, or to exploit. He has little patience with the intellectual traditions that see wild places as mere backdrops for human subjectivity or resources to be extracted. Throughout *Song at the Year's Turning* human endeavour is mocked or trumped by 'long erosion of the green tide'. And Thomas will pick up this theme again, notably in *Poetry for Supper* (1958) where he will once again address Prytherch ('Even while you sleep / In your low room, the dark moor exerts / Its pressure on the timbers') and in *Tares* (1961) where even more explicitly:

> slow but surely
> Green blades were brandished, the old triumph
> Of nature over the brief violence
> Of man

Nature is not sublime for Thomas. Its 'triumph' is one not of glorious resurgence but of insidious undermining. His is a proto-necropastoral vision of entropy, decay and distortion; of barren moors and blighting frosts, or the haywire fecundity of bramble and gorse.

I *love* this about Thomas. I love it not merely for its lack of sentimentality, but for the way it speaks forcefully back to the racialised ecologies of Wales as conjured by the English imagination. As Thomas writes in his 1946 essay 'Some Contemporary Scottish Writing':

> What is Wales after all, but a kind of western country that is not worth bothering about apart from its scenery and its natural resources? Wild Wales! Yes, but it all resides in the landscape.

Thomas's representation of nature counteracts not only the lingering cult of the picturesque in English lyric imagination, but also a politics of cultural subordination that renders Wales as *merely* a landscape and consequently as a peripheral site of residual culture. If the English lyric imagination sought to transform Wales into some kind of quasi-mystical refuge from the pressures of the modern political centre, Thomas strove to show us that their so-called sanctuary was haunted by unquiet (perhaps even hostile) forces.

Scotland (and Ireland) have also been on the receiving end of this representational strategy, a hangover from the Romantic lyric tradition in which Nature (capital N) is a source of spiritual awakening or succour. In this view of the world Nature is the sublime other; it is a view that assumes an over-simplified and frictionless distinction between human beings and their environment, and it renders what takes place within wild or rural contexts as meaningful only in terms of its interaction with and on human subjectivity. Crucially, this fixation on the beauty of the 'landscape' becomes a kind of tacit justification for the acts of colonisation, exploitation, and extraction that take place there. This process is material, but it is also imaginative: the land is plundered of its riches both mineral and aesthetic. Generations of English artists appropriate rural Wales, converting both land and lives into dusty lyric freight. Thomas tackles this directly in 'A Welsh Testament', which appears in *Tares* and is worth quoting at length:

> And always there was their eyes' strong
> Pressure on me: You are Welsh, they said;
> Speak to us so; keep your fields free
> Of the smell of petrol, the loud roar
> Of hot tractors; we must have peace
> And quietness.
>
> Is a museum
> Peace? I asked. Am I keeper
> Of the heart's relics, blowing the dust
> In my own eyes?

It is not, of course, that Thomas is any great supporter of 'hot tractors'; what he skewers here is colonial hypocrisy; these entitled emissaries from a world of toxic extraction and mechanised destruction, insisting – as if these 'outposts' exist for their benefit – that the rural be kept 'pure', tied to anachronistic forms of life and labour so much the better to preserve an idyll of rural retreat for those who claim the comforts of the centre while demanding unfettered access to the compensations of the edge. Or, as my Grandfather – a man in the Prytherch mould – once put it: 'They won't let you have the nothing you were born to in peace.'

Thomas (like my Grandfather) refuses the idea of the countryside as an infinitely accessible leisure space, a picturesque resource to be tapped by those who refuse to see the entangled relationships between the urban and the rural; the complex dynamics of hierarchy and suppression in which they themselves are enmeshed. If the idea of rural Wales is aligned in the English imagination with a flight from the pressures of city living, it is also a site of abdication from social responsibility; an effectively depoliticised zone in which spatial and moral separation from one's broader human community are wilfully conflated. If Wild Wales is an escape from the settled, conventional (English) centre, then Wild Wales is suffered to survive only because it helps this centre to hold. Thomas is having *none* of that.

Thomas was having none of it to the extent that he became a vocal supporter of the Meibion Glyndwr (Sons of Glyndwr) group, which carried out arson attacks against English-owned holiday cottages in rural Wales, particularly throughout the '70s and '80s. In an interview in 1998 he made the following statement in support of this particular brand of dangerous direct action: 'What is one death against the death of the whole Welsh nation?' This might strike us as a shocking comment for a lifelong pacifist to make, but I'd argue that there's slightly more to it than simple nationalistic tub-thumping. I think we can read Thomas's support for the Sons of Glyndwr in the context of a profound conviction that imperialism – and modern capitalist imperialism in particular – is the initiating trauma and foundational ill from which all other evils (including warfare) spring. For Thomas, the Welsh nation is not just a culturally distinct political territory but a last spiritual redoubt against an existential threat and a great moral evil.

We see this in the poems, and in Prytherch in particular, who survives not only the attrition of the elements but the appropriation of the colonising gaze. *He* is a 'fortress' impregnable, unavailable to Romantic pastoral projections. *He* will not be quaint or safe or wise or spiritually uplifting. *He* remains impervious to any outward attempts at meaning-making, even (especially) from Thomas himself.

This vision of Welsh land and of the Welsh hill people was shaped by the war, but also by the bare-hard years of pre-war depression. For Thomas, and for an entire cohort of Welsh writers – writers such as Huw Menai and Alun Lewis – the dogged persistence of Welsh tradition, land, and language had (as M Wynn Thomas notes) 'paradoxically metamorphosed into proofs of invincible endurance'. The unyielding antiquity of the Welsh landscape becomes a warrant of survival, inextricably linked to what – for want of a better word – we'll call the Welsh soul.

All very rousing, says a sceptical friend of mine, *but Thomas wrote poetry in English, don't forget.* He gives me a look when he says this, the unspoken meaning of which is *and you write poetry in English, don't forget.* As if I could. As if Thomas ever did. Nailing the unique discomfort of the Anglo-Welsh writer, Thomas describes his position as: 'neither one thing nor the other. He keeps going in a no-man's land between the two cultures'. More forcefully, in his 1964 lecture 'Words and the Poet' Thomas specifically addresses this conflicted attitude towards his upbringing and education: 'One of the first questions that arises for a Welshman face to face with the English tongue is: What is my true feeling for these words? Am I fascinated, repelled, resentful? [...] Where he has a real love and respect for his native traditions, he will regret his enforced separation from them, and resent the necessity of having to use words, which to all intents and purposes are those of a foreign people. [...] I mention that as personally applicable.' In 'The Old Language', first published in *The Stones of the Field*, Thomas asks directly within the space of a short lyric: 'England, what have you done to make the speech / My fathers used a stranger at my lips, / An offence to the ear, a shackle on the tongue [?]'

I know this accusation and this ache. And I can't, when I think of Thomas in this context, not also think of Stephen Dedalus in James Joyce's *Portrait of the Artist as a Young Man* (1916). Educated in the language and nice habits of English / the English, Stephen nevertheless feels that this language can only be for him 'an acquired speech' under which he must inwardly bristle and chafe. Yet, if he is imperfectly assimilated by and into the English tongue, his fluency in English performs a kind of separation – an enforced exile – from his own people. Damned from both sides, doubly excluded. In *The Wretched of the Earth* (1961) Franz Fanon levels this uncompromising assessment:

> At the very moment when the native intellectual is anxiously trying to create a cultural work he fails to realise that he is utilising techniques and language which are borrowed from the stranger in his country. He contents himself with stamping these instruments with a hallmark which he wishes to be national, but which is strangely reminiscent of exoticism. The native intellectual who comes back to his people by way of cultural achievements behaves in fact like a foreigner. [...] The culture that the intellectual leans toward is often no more than a stock of particularisms. He wishes to attach himself to the people; but instead he only catches hold of their outer garments.

I found myself wondering if this were true of Thomas, and if this were true of myself. The sting is particularly sharp because (certainly in Thomas's case) the literary culture into which he enters labours with feverish industry to both assimilate and estrange him, to persistently figure him as 'other' but to defuse any potential threat such outsider status might contain. We see this in the transmission and reception of Thomas's early work – that interminable insistence upon his 'local' Welsh identity.

In his introduction to *Song at the Year's Turning* no less a person than John Betjeman described Thomas as 'essentially a local poet', thus recuperating him into an acceptable colonial form. John Press, writing in his introduction to the anthology *Map of Modern English Verse* (1969), dismisses Thomas's first three books as being 'printed by small, little-known firms in Wales', going on to condescendingly locate his work within 'the small world of the Welsh hill country'. Again, in the anthology *The Voice of Poetry* (1950), we see Thomas described as 'a clergyman in the Welsh hill country' writing in a style of 'lyrical simplicity [...] His range is not wide but his vision is penetrating...' At least he got 'penetrating', but it's obvious to anyone with eyes in their head that such framing heightens the colonial tension between Thomas's 'small world' of Wales and the broader British arena within which it has been located. And 'simplicity'? As if to reassure themselves (and us) that nothing rural in its concerns could prove threatening or disruptive to the metropolitan centre.

Poor Thomas. I felt for him. But my friend says *Poor nothing*, says, *you know he sent his kids to elite public school, don't you... In England.* After his death in 2000, obituaries were full of this kind of sentiment: Thomas as a man 'riddled' with 'contradictions': the ardent Welsh nationalist and advocate of the Welsh language who never wrote poetry in Welsh; the devout Anglican priest whose poetry wrestled with and frequently apostrophised an uncomfortably elusive God; who was supposed to have burnt his cassock on the beach at Aberdaron upon retirement from the church. These articles gave us Thomas the inhospitable 'Ogre of Wales', so set against the Machine – as he called it – of Mammon and modernity that he lived in an increasingly uncomfortable series of vicarages, stone crofts without heat or electric light, damp on the walls, a morbid recluse, half Victor Meldrew, half Ted Kaczynski. We see him as a man without small-talk, and so set against the sociality of his fellows that he'd sooner camp in the garden than sleep under the roof of an acquaintance. These stories are told in incredulous tones. We're invited to laugh at the crotchety comic-book ridiculousness of Thomas, but also to repudiate him as an obvious phoney. For 'contradictions' read 'hypocrisy'. I am not so sure about that.

To begin with, to me sleeping outside seems infinitely preferable to the claustrophobic social awkwardness of hedged hospitality – that's by-the-by, but I am starting to suspect that I am exactly the same kind of curmudgeon as Thomas – and I can't help wondering if laughing at Thomas performs a similar function to the persistent 'small world' framing of his work: a way of defusing or discrediting the implied social challenge contained within his radically renunciate lifestyle. I also find myself reading Thomas and his uneasy habitation of the unhomely home that is English through the lens of Homi K Bhabha and his exploration of the 'unhomely' in The Location of Culture (1994): for the post-colonial subject, to be unhomely is to feel not-at-home in any particular experience, often – ironically – within one's own homeland. It is also an experience that troubles the fixed boundaries of one's world, so that 'the borders between home and world become hopelessly confused'. What Bhabha means by this is that the colonial subject becomes unable to dissociate their home from its political and cultural context; the private psychic sphere is contaminated and encroached upon by one's public dimension. Certainly, as Fflur Dafydd has noted, this can be applied to Thomas, caught between the Welsh *home* and the Welsh *nation*.

His later poems absolutely bear the marks of this uncertain self, of shifting, often fractalised identity. In 'Reflections' from *No Truce With The Furies* (1995), the speaker contemplates his own face as a 'white flag', yet the truce it tenders is ignored by the Furies, who are 'at home / in the mirror; it is *their* address' (emphasis mine), a place the speaker comes to not in order to confirm some essential truth of their personality but to 'partake of a shifting / identity never your own'. In many ways, 'Reflections' can be read as a culmination of anxieties and preoccupations expressed throughout Thomas's career. In *The Echoes Return Slow* (1988), a brief poetic fragment poses the question:

In a dissolving
world what certainties
for the self, whose identity
is its performance?
You have no address,
says life, and your destination
is where you began.

The lines drift apart across the blank space of the page, creating a porous, unsettled terrain. There is something spectral about it, the words (and the identity they evoke) have not coalesced into a definite shape; everything is possible, infinitely susceptible, and nothing is decided.

The Echoes Return Slow is a project of doubleness and division. Published just three years after *Neb* (a more traditional autobiography – albeit written with typical layers of Thomasian distance and evasiveness, in the third person), it shifts between dense prose and razor-fine poems to create a double narrative that enacts Thomas's dualities. It is as if the text itself were divided, and this division becomes for Thomas a way to reinvent poetic method. Perhaps this is what Thomas was always moving towards, a way to challenge the assumption that duality is something disabling, and instead transform it into a kind of restlessly interrogative radical ambivalence. In 'Genealogy' (*Tares*, 1961) he is not yet there, but the poem proliferates images of multiple, mutating identities, each connected through a sense of displacement and isolation: 'I stand now / In the hard light of the brief day / Without roots, but with many branches'. Who can resist a comparison to those early Prytherch poems, Thomas's inscrutable hill farmer figured as a tree 'Enduring' under 'the curious stars'?

In 'A Welshman at St James's Park' which first appeared in *Pieta* (1966), the poet is still grappling with this double sense of exclusion. The piece sees the speaker transplanted to the metropolitan centre, at odds with the manicured lawns and the mediated experience of nature they imply. There is a realisation – a reckoning – in this circumscribed green city space, and the poem introduces a note of panic: 'I am not one / Of the public; I have come a long way / To realise it'. I find myself moved by this piece and the lonely superiority of the figure at its centre. Was this the moment that Thomas realised the cage of being other to everyone, neither one thing nor another? It's the word 'public' that shakes me up: the speaker is not merely excluded *from* wider community, but incarcerated *within* his own head. I know *that* feeling too.

But this perpetual at-oddness has its compensations. In a 1990 interview, Thomas remembered a piece of advice given to him by Saunders Lewis: 'I complained once [...] about the tension of writing in one language and wanting to speak another and his reply was that out of such tensions art was born.' Contemplating these 'tensions' allows us not only to read his work more fully, but also to read Thomas's self-dramatising contradictions, to read his legend.

In his essay 'Of Mimicry and Man' (1984), Bhabha suggests that mimicry is a not merely an aping of oppressor aesthetics (with varying degrees of consciousness) but rather a tactic to imitate and disrupt the colonial norm, and as such a key part of the transferral of power. For the colonised their – our – doing of English undoes it. Our presence inside of English renders English itself strange, and while this inevitably involves a threat to the subjectivity of the colonised, it also entails an equal and opposite threat to the stability of imperial power.

My friend is not convinced, but that's alright. Thomas doesn't exist to convince you. He exists to train us in ambiguity, in the value of doubt and discomfort, which are, in their best sense, a form of seeking, a desire to communicate and to know. Not unlike the God that haunts his poetry – sometimes oppressively present and sometimes painfully absent – there is much that must remain unspoken, that has no language – in English *or* in Welsh – that therefore must remain unknown. It is up to us to come to an accommodation with that as best we can. 🌿 **FL**

Arts

Our irregular arts strands include:

Insidious Fire – ON FILM

Credibly Agile – ON DANCE

All This Fiddle – ON MUSIC

Some Untidy Spot – ON VISUAL ART

These Phenomena Are Important – ON TECH

A. Driver, a driver

Writing a poem is not an inherently cinematic business: give or take a broken quill, wind-snatched page or virused computer, it offers little by way of visual drama. It's no surprise that most films about poetry stick to the salacious parts of the poet's life, relegating the poems to an unfortunate aside. *Paterson* (written and directed by Jim Jarmusch, with poems by Ron Padgett) is different. Amazon describes it thus: 'Paterson is a bus driver in the city of Paterson, New Jersey – they share the name. He's also a poet, recording his daily observations and thoughts in the form of beautiful prose.' Alright to be a poet then, so long as he only writes prose.

Adam Driver's Paterson is modest, reserved, concerned and fastidious: we might think of him as the 'Pedestrian Bus Driver'. He folds his clothes, has Cheerios every weekday morning, likes his wife, eats what she cooks him (even the cheddar and brussels sprouts pie), has a house just like his neighbours' houses and, most crucially, a job that isn't teaching Creative Writing in a university. He reads William Carlos Williams and the poets of the New York School, and writes like they do, in praise of the incidental, quotidian and downbeat. The first poem in the film is about Ohio Blue Tip Matches, and the poetry never really inflates itself into anything more esoteric or abstract.

Not exactly an action thriller then, despite the bus chase potential of our hero's day job. The most narratively fizzy moments of the film are when Paterson's bus breaks down, when a spurned lover pulls a toy pistol in the bar, and when the dog eats his oeuvre. Throughout, Paterson remains calm, gentle and unerringly kind. To Paterson's wife Laura, played by Golshifteh Farahani, falls the whimsy and 'originality' of the conventional Hollywood protagonist poet. She may look stunning in every shot but she overspends, cooks food inedible to anyone not in love with her, buys a fancy guitar so she can be a country-and-western star, and dreams of her husband riding a silver elephant in ancient Persia. She's also warm-hearted and lovely, and believes her husband's poems to be the most beautiful things in the world. To an outsider (even us), Laura looks like the creative one. And it's not that she's not creative; it's just that Paterson's own, much less-blatant, creativity is recognised only by whatever other poets he happens upon. The role of poetry in the film is to keep faith with the lived world, to observe experience just as haiku do, and to still time in their way. Paterson writes honest, bare-boned poems, and does so quietly. The thought of him reading them in public or assuming any of the confidence or self-indulgence of the (so-called) public poet is very clearly a thought that hasn't occurred to either the character or the film.

But *Paterson* isn't really a film about a poet: it's a film that wants to be a poem, and very often is. There's something quietly, intrinsically poetic about how it uses form and imagery, and in how it distrusts not just hyperbole and drama, but also the usual narrative impulse towards story arc and resolution. This is a film that rhymes, not just the perfect rhyme of protagonist's name and location (and William Carlos Williams's book title), or the character's profession and the leading man's surname, but the visual rhyme between recurring sets of twins and recurring sets of pairs of people talking behind him on his bus. It also rhymes time; every morning rhyming with how the previous one began, every evening closing with the same beer in the same bar. Repetition and refrain are used as patterning narrative devices but, just as Paterson admires how the black circles Laura paints on the white shower curtain all look a bit different, change occurs, of course it does, and what changes is language as the words of his poems evolve. That's it? No character development, no narrative arc, no tragedy, no sex, no violence, no drugs, no catastrophe, no natural disaster, no heroics, no bank heist, no hit-and-run, no infidelity, no death, not even a mild heart attack? That's it. What we get is a sense of how a poet's mind might actually work when the only splash it's trying to make is a splash of language, and even that is more a curated drop than a whole, spilling paint tin.

And if this magazine were a scene in *Paterson*, this section would now close out with a close-up of a tin on a shelf or the barman's hand drying a pint glass. Or Paterson's knee. Or Laura's hair in a plume against the pillow, and our point of view would be fused with his, very simply watching her sleep. 🥀 **VG**

Paterson (dir Jim Jarmusch, 2016)

Insidious Fire

Pretty Woman

The part where Richard Gere
takes her to the opera to satisfy
himself that she has a soul.
Remember, it's *La Traviata*,
all tragedy in heady Paris.
Vivian's shoulders are heavenly
in that red siren dress.
This is Gere gently taking
her pulse and attentive to the gulp
in the beautiful throat,
a quiver on those sumptuous lips.   ❧ MA

Pretty Woman (dir Garry Marshall, 1993)

All This Fiddle

What rhymes with 'Unstoppable Sex Machine'?

Two things happened to me the other day, arriving from different universes and now lodged at the same neural address. Thing One: I turned up at work to find that my department was to be dissolved and my job was for the chop, together with that of hundreds of friends and colleagues across the arts, humanities and social sciences. Thing Two: a copy of Jim Bob's *Where Songs Come From* came in the post. If you weren't around in the early '90s, Jim Bob (James Morrison) was the singer and lyricist of post-punk japesters Carter the Unstoppable Sex Machine. *Where Songs Come From* is a collection of lyrics to 150 songs, interleaved with anecdotes, essays on craft and autobiographical excursions.

There's spooky action at work here. The abrupt restructuring of my university – an unhomely home in which we've built and sustained good things, things we believe in – was accompanied by all the usual bad-faith euphemism and aspirational grift (you know: *rationalize our portfolio* for *lay off staff*). We were introduced to some expensive new brand guidelines, together with pointers on the tone of voice we ought to adopt, the better to embody said brand. We were also exposed to a lot of overinflated abstracts: *excellence, innovation, global thinking, co-creation*. That sort of thing.

I mention these two in the same breath – institutional bromides and Morrison's lyrics – because the phrase *excellence, innovation, global thinking, co-creation* might have been lifted from a Carter song (you can in fact sing it to the listy bit of 'Anytime Anyplace Anywhere'). This is because Morrison has an affinity for lists, and particularly for lists that bowl along under their own momentum, landing on all the rhymes and points of rhythmic congruence:

I've never been insane or put my baby on a plane
With a suitcase that's alive and ticking
And Your Honour, I confess that I've never tasted meths
Or hid a gun in a box of fried chicken

Also for rhyme in general, and in particular for a killer opening couplet:

Sheriff Fatman started out in business as a granny farmer.
He was infamous for fifteen minutes and he appeared on
    Panorama.

Or just the balls-out ostentation of rhyming 'Mirror, Signal and Manoeuvre' with 'Glory, Glory, Hallelujah'. Morrison offers a winsome account of his rhyming in the fourth essay ('A Big Book of Rhymes'):

> I'd rather not be caught staring into the hushed middle distance at the funeral of a close friend or family member, as I go through the alphabet in my head, in search of a word to follow Amarillo – billo, cillo, dillo, fillo, gillo, and so on, before I move on to near rhymes like hero and zero, until I settle on something clever – armadillo for instance, or Michael Portillo. Then of course I'd need to work out how to justify Michael Portillo's inclusion in a song about asking for directions to a city in Texas.

In fact, the book's full of solid advice and examples for writers of all stripes. On intertextuality ('I hope there's no copyright on humming'); on word choice ('I will always choose the best words available to me. If they're swearwords, I'll use them'); on influence ('When you've written enough songs, you eventually become your own main influence. You start to sound like you.')

The most useful instruction is exemplified in the lyrics themselves: Carter songs were known for their wordplay, a mix of inveterate punning, bathos, and turns on popular titles ('The Only Living Boy in New Cross'; 'Born on the 5th of November'). They exhibit a particular attraction to corrupted language: that of advertising, brand management, sloganeering, cliché, and the like. (There's a fun bit where Morrison draws up an imaginary concept album, the titles all drawn from supermarket jingles.) Collectively, they make for an oeuvre committed to meddling and mischief-making; if people are going to dick around with language, you dick around with it right back. But there's loving homage here too, and Morrison will pick up and play with anything that catches his ear: the hymn, the football chant, Shakespeare, the lyrics of other songwriters (though he will only thieve, he is at pains to point out, from songs he loves).

On several occasions Morrison deals in misquotations and misattributed wisdom, with zero interest in verifying origins or originals ('This pedantry is interrupting the flow of the story') It's an attitude that foregrounds language-as-used: what it's used for, and why, and by whom, and how it means to work on us. His own sources, cited anecdotally, become increasingly implausible as the book goes on ('My Shakespearean scholar friend, Viennetta'; 'My made-up actor friend, Henry'). This is a fun gag, but also an earnest one; it amounts to something like: You know why you're here, and I know why you're here, do you really need to know who first said imitation was the sincerest form of flattery? You don't, do you.

Thing One and Thing Two are so *unlike* that they click together with the lovely click of a good rhyme. Thing One: disingenuousness dolled up as pragmatism. Thing Two: sincerity masquerading as mischief. Sing it with me:

excellence, innovation, global thinking, co-creation

There's a great phrase towards the end of *Where Songs Come From*, one of Morrison's own coinages: the four earworms of the apocalypse. I'm having that, and I feel certain Morrison won't mind. ❦ AP

Where Songs Come From by Jim Bob (Cherry Red Books, 2025; £40)

From Connie Converse, with no return address

Dimple: it is nice to hear from you,
in the swell-swab indigo of the underside
of my parked car.

I have become afraid of small things,
although not you, my dear. Just, my guitar
lies untuned, as I can no longer stand the pegs.

I hear you in the bettle-chimes
of the empty I'm becoming
newly accustomed to.

I should like us
to keep in touch, although
it does not feel likely.

Have you ever felt as if you're filled
with fleas or pumpkinseed? I have lost
my sense of smell. I have lost

my new pack of ink cartridges, my cig-
arettes. Oh well. It was good to think of you.   ❦ **AB**

How Sad, How Lovely by Connie Converse (Lau Derette Record-
ings, 2009); To Anyone Who Ever Asks: The Life, Music, and Mys-
tery of Connie Converse by Howard Fishman (Wildfire, 2023; £25)

Some Untidy Spot

Napalm & magpies

John Akomfrah (b. 1957) helmed the British Pavilion at the most recent Venice Art Biennale. His commission, *Listening All Night To The Rain*, stretched the term 'mixed-media' around hundreds of sources, all playing simultaneously on dozens of screens in seven dark rooms. He titled the rooms *Canto II, III, IV, V, VI, VII, VIII. Canto I*, meanwhile, is the name for the show projected onto the front wall, with a somewhat politically redacted nod to Ezra Pound in the accompanying text (which glancingly addresses him, without actually quoting from his *The Cantos*).

It feels like this:

You walk in. You are surrounded by screens showing 19th-century portrait photography and rusted scissors, filmed underwater in a fast-running shallow stream. Dark purple walls. Upstairs, red walls. Room full of retro music technology hanging from the ceiling in a massive net. Profundity in gold Times New Roman on the red wall. (Later, you check online, and discover it is from an experimental composer's Facebook page; part of a guided meditation from 2020). Spools of tape and blank CDs hang down like chandeliers. Black walls, red curtain, six screens showing enormous ships sliding down slipways to the sea. One from Newfoundland, one from Northern England. Cut: crowd of old men in flat caps and woollen coats. British moor; drystone walls, mist. More moors, more mist. Blasted trees. Orange-jacketed man, long-view. Rubber ducks in an ocean from six angles. Same man, close up. Shirtless African soldiers. Biafran War. Man lying down. Body of a child in a coffin on the back of a pushbike. Overfull bus in Africa. Long line of women walking with objects on their heads. Translation of Chinese poem containing the exhibition's title. A woman in a cot. Photographs of James Baldwin, Malcolm X, civil rights leaders. Orange walls. East Asian woman in fuchsia nehru jacket in mossy pine-grove. Same woman, from above, on picnic blanket. Old-fashioned music equipment, small trumpet. Flyover footage of napalm hitting palm forest. East Asian children in traditional dress wiping blood from their faces. Back to picnic shot. You walk out into the bright Venice sun.

❦

Venice is a magpie city: Greek bronze and Roman porphyry adorning Gothic arches atop Byzantine columns housing Egyptian relics in an island labyrinth full of all the world's loot. Pound's *The Cantos* is a magpie poem: Italian memories in Classical frames in American language surrounding Chinese characters in an unfinished frame filled with all a man's thoughts. *Listening All Night To The Rain*, in its appropriation of superficial elements from *The Cantos*, aspires to accumulate it as one more source among its hundreds. (That the titular phrase from 11th-century Chinese poet Su Shi – also known as Su Tung-P'o, Su Dong-Po, or Su Dongpo – is also the title of the most recent translation, which happens to be the only one published to spell his name as the installation does, 'Su Dongpo', and that the printed poem also adorns that translation's back-cover, draws some suspicion about just how deeply these things were evaluated before they were appropriated.)

This, however, does not matter to the audience. The relevant question is not one of depth, but of resolution: how many sources can be forced into a frame before their inclusion becomes a cheap and clumsy thing, and the signal is lost in the noise?

In the accompanying text:

Listening All Night To The Rain positions various theories of 'acoustemology': a portmanteau combining 'acoustic' and 'epistemology' coined by ethnomusicologist Steven Feld that denotes the study of how the sonic experience mirrors and shapes our cultural realities. The soundtracks to each of the *Cantos* layer together archival material with field recordings, speeches, popular and devotional music in order to extend the sense of hybridity in the filmic collages and reflect upon the multiplicity inherent in cultural identity more broadly.

The word 'acoustemology' functions as a good example. 'Acoustic' is preserved; 'episteme' is not. It is not a functional portmanteau without an accompanying explanation: on this model, it is apparent why the plunderphonic sound collage does not, actually, reproduce all the meaning of its parts. If a fox eats a half-dozen hedgehogs, the contents of his stomach will not reveal each of their single big things.

The woman in the mist of the Asian pine-grove, standing still, has to be distilled by the viewer in five seconds; the term for this is of course 'stereotype'. Orientalist appeal to a mystical retreat. This contrasts with the napalming of a different, but equally familiar, kind of Asian forest the same way a lorry contrasts with a pedestrian. War is terrible, the East is serene, we've seen all these images before, but for the sake of collage artists everywhere, give thanks there is still some force in a firebomb.

When a musician plays every note at once, the result is certainly loud, but it is also mostly incomprehensible. A temporary exhibition in a square crowded with other large temporary exhibitions does not permit the attention necessary to digest anywhere near this amount of information; therefore, we might conclude that the intended effect is precisely the kind of bewilderment that the discordant orchestra produces. I am thrilled that the British Arts Council are happy to make people uncomfortable – if, however, this is the sole intention of a piece, I might prefer that something more difficult than discomfort (which could have been quite easily achieved with only one video, the difficult-to-reckon-with inclusion of a child's dead body being carried down a dirt-track) was prioritised.

Juxtaposition is a powerful tool. Working with pre-existing material, it is almost the only tool; these pieces are not made, but arranged. It is difficult, sometimes, to know if accumulation of sources constitutes a whole artistic method, or produces a whole artistic effect; this is alright. The effect, every time, is a slightly weaker sense of bewilderment. Moments of force emerge, of course; but the threshold for shock exponentially grows. The number of images makes what would be grotesque and clumsy alone seem subtle. Dilution is a kind of curation.

The internet's natural patterns of usage have made this experience of horror beside the picturesque quotidian; on a big screen, in another juxtapositional frame in a crowded square of national efforts, it is still occasionally arresting. Akomfrah's magpie curation is certainly Poundian in form, but since video can reproduce entirely and seamlessly what verse can reproduce only perspectivally and with great effort, their effects are very different; I did not feel I had encountered any kind of through-line, or story. The video-artist, as opposed to the filmmaker, is reliant entirely on associations the onlooker already has. Not dramatic, but historical. Another snipped quote from Bachelard here, another piece of military archive footage there, the illusion of some big force just beneath the surface of so many disjunct exempla. My own snipped quote from Bachelard, to cap things off, and illuminate the inadequacy of curation for radical statements: 'If you want to move beyond history... you'll discover that calendars for future lives must be made with history's old images.' ❦ **RMA**

Listening All Night to the Rain by John Akomfrah,
60th International Art Exhibition, La Biennale di Venezia, Italy,
April 20th – November 24th 2024

Write for us!

It is free to submit to *The Little Review* and always will be. We are open for submissions for roughly a third of the year, in three six-week windows. Our next windows are:

❧ June 1st – July 13th
❧ September 1st – October 13th
❧ January 15th – February 28th

Our submission guidelines are quite unusual. Please read them carefully before sending work (thelittlereview.co.uk/submit). If you would prefer to avoid the internet, our postal address is: *The Little Review*, 56 St Paul's Terrace, York, YO24 4BJ

Insolence
& Triviality

Mailbox

Second-hand advice

To the Editor: Asked to contribute some thoughts to the magazine *Seventeen* in 1963, Marianne Moore produced a little essay, 'Profit is a Dead Weight' – 'a sentence I happened upon in my Italian dictionary: *lucro è peso morto*' – which concludes:

> Example is needed, not counsel; but let me submit here these four precepts:
> - Feed imagination food that invigorates.
> - Whatever it is, do it with all your might.
> - Never do to another what you would not wish done to yourself.
> - Say to yourself, 'I will be responsible.'
> Put these principles to the test, and you will be inconvenienced by being overtrusted, overbefriended, overconsulted, half adopted, and have no leisure. Face that when you come to it.

Good luck.
Ian Sansom

Being flightless, man throws rocks at birds

To the Editor: When PJ Kavanagh was introduced to Patrick Kavanagh, the latter glared at him and snarled 'change your name!' Same applies here. There already is a *Little Review*, as it happens; and yours can only be a wren trying to soar on the back of an eagle. The ghosts of Apollinaire, Aragon, Barnes, Breton, Cocteau, Colum, Crane, 'HD', Eliot, Ford, Joyce, Lewis, Pound, Stein, Stevens, Tzara, Williams and Yeats – and dozens of others – will haunt you.

    Yours sincerely,
    Harry Gilonis

[For more on names, see 'Marx, Duck & the boneyard', pp.3-6, an article written several days before we received the encouraging letter above – Ed]

Lugworm casts

Meta!

To the Editor: There should be more aphorisms about aphorisms. They are under-aphorised.

    Every aphorism comes with a sense of authority that its author doesn't possess. Aphorisms appear to make solids of thoughts which are in fact gaseous or liquid.

    Aphorisms are like gallstones or kidney stones: at best annoying, at worst painful, but whatever they are, they're calcified versions of substances not meant to be solid. Aphorisms are like lugworm casts or coprolites: hardened leavings.

    What are aphorisms? Heaps of stones on the top of a hill. A cairn at best, or a way-marker.

    Yours faithfully,
    Adrian Masters

ittle Crossword

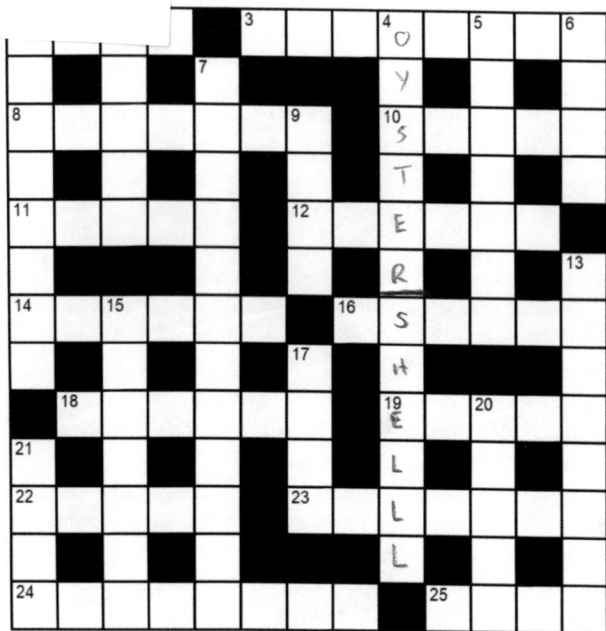

The first person to send a correct set of answers to 56 St Paul's Terrace, York, YO24 4BJ or mailbox@thelittlereview.co.uk will receive a box of chocolates or handful of recent books. Indicate your preferred prize when submitting your answers. No search engines! Google is so tawdry. If stuck, consult a library, a librarian or a well-read friend.

Across

1 One of Shakespeare's feet *(4)*

3 Characteristic of or pertaining to Old Possum? *(8)*

8 Cressida's lover *(7)*

10 Heraldic colour – Pyrrhus' arms, in *Hamlet* *(5)*

11 The third to tell a story in the *Canterbury Tales* *(5)*

12 When 'blood hath been shed', according to Macbeth *(3,3)*

14 'Yet never was the _____ nation without poetry' (Sidney) *(6)*

16 Science fiction writer, deviser of the Three Laws of Robotics *(6)*

18 '_____ thee, witch', in both Shakespeare and John Ashbery *(6)*

19 Scottish poet Muir *(5)*

22 The worst beast in Baudelaire's 'menagerie of vices' *(5)*

23 Mozart's rival in *Amadeus* *(7)*

24 Tragic heroine – Oedipus' daughter *(8)*

25 'What his common sense came short, / He _____ out wi' law, man' *(4)*

Down

1 Type of rhyme, e.g. in Hopkins's 'And all is seared with trade; bleared, smeared with toil' *(8)*

2 Modernist Marianne *(5)*

4 In the 3ac mode, what piles up in 'sawdust restaurants'... *(6-6)*

5 ...and what are 'lilacs', in his 'Portrait of a Lady'? *(2,5)*

6 'What oft was thought, but _____ so well expressed' *(4)*

7 The method of Langland, Bunyan, and Orwell? (-ing not -al) *(12)*

9 'The sound should _____ an echo to the sense' *(4)*

13 A 'singer everyone has heard', according to Robert Frost *(4,4)*

15 Noble title of Walter Scott and Walter Elliot *(7)*

17 Soul singer who tried a little tenderness? (first name only) *(4)*

20 _____ of the Deutschland, in Hopkins *(5)*

21 WB Yeats's 'staggering girl' *(4)*　　　　　🐝 BP

Interview

...d with
K Patrick

K Patrick was one of 20 writers on *Granta*'s once-a-decade list, The Best of Young British Novelists, in 2023. Born and living in Scotland, Patrick is the author of the novel *Mrs S* (2023), which follows a young, Australian butch matron at a boarding school who is drawn into an affair with the headmaster's wife, and the poetry collection *Three Births* (2024). A second novel, *Sid*, is supposedly forthcoming in February 2026, unless Patrick misses the publisher's deadline, which judging from the following conversation is a distinct possibility. Patrick has a buzz-cut, a friendly manner, and an unsettling habit of redirecting questions back at the interviewer. Parts of this interview have been edited for brevity, edited out of a sense of mischief, or omitted because the dictaphone stopped working and I was enjoying the conversation too much to notice. (There was a great bit about the sensuality of TS Eliot's *Four Quartets*. Alas, you'll never read it.)

I've heard you write in bed.
All the time. I was doing it until about an hour and a half ago.

How does that help?
In bed, the stakes are extremely low. If I was to get up and put a different outfit on and sit at a desk, I'd freak out. I'd think *this is too serious*. Writing in bed works for me because it means I'm able to get some privacy back, for me and my pleasure, to make writing more of a selfish act, to ask: is this entertaining *me*, is this meaningful to *me*?

As long as the lighting is low and I've got my duvet and pillows and my pyjamas – or sometimes not even pyjamas – it feels like it's easier. I'll have my notebooks with me, like 10 books spread out across the bed.

I do *have* a desk, I just hardly ever sit at it. Sometimes for editing. But even then, sometimes I like to do it when I'm sleepy – there's just something about that state. I'll start working between 5am and 7am. Those are my favourite times to work, it's a detached time, the squishy part of the day. It's the best time of day because it's not *real* yet, the world isn't a particular place yet between five and seven… later on, I can't write because the day's too real – I have to put washing on, or do something important.

Do you ever fall back to sleep while writing?
No, writing really wires me. I can't even read before bed because I get overexcited… If I want to get a good night's sleep I've got to go to bed at eight. It's difficult to maintain a social life if you go to bed early.

Well, writing in bed worked for Proust. And I believe that for

a long time he went to bed early.
But *how* early? Some of my friends go to bed at 11 and are like 'what an early night!' but I've been asleep for three hours by then.

How's your second novel coming along?
Slowly. Everyone warned me second novels are extremely difficult. They were right.

What's it about?
It's about more gays! [*Laughs*] I don't really know what it's about. In fact, I wrote that in my notebook today: WHAT IS THIS ABOUT? I want to return to the themes I've been working over, like masculinity, this idea of a queer rural, or what it means to be queer in rural areas, and the body. But what it's *about* remains to be seen.

OK. Where is it set?
It's set in Scotland. There's a specific place, but I'm still deciding on whether or not to use the placename... There are all these huge decisions that I have to make in the next couple of months because I'm nearing the deadline.

When's your publisher's deadline?
In seven weeks.

Oh dear. Have you figured out the plot yet?
It has a plot this time! *Mrs S* got accused of being plotless, which I think was mean, because there was *definitely* a plot in it. But in this one I'm trying to do Big Plot, so we'll see how that turns out. It's fun, it just isn't always how I usually think – I don't enter into

a project with an idea of beginning, middle and end.

In the new issue of a much larger magazine, *The Erotic Review*, you write: 'The body is too good for the poem.'
Yes, I *did* write that. What does it mean? Nine times out of 10 in my work I'm writing into this failure of language... The body *is* too good for the poem. Especially the queer body, the trans body.

Why especially?
Because you're on the outside of language – in a good way, though obviously it's used against the trans body in a lot of ways. The way language operates currently doesn't quite cover the trans body in the way it should, or the available terminology isn't there. Language can feel like an attempt to clarify, but when it comes to transness I feel like I want to mystify, or re-mystify, or keep it mysterious somehow.

Writing about sex is famously difficult. Maybe sex is when we're most aware of our bodies, and furthest from language.
I think that's fair. I also think language is prone to ruining those things really easily. When you actually put words on the page it has this awful sense of permanence, whereas sex is the opposite of that... Sex writing is a real test of an author's ability.

The PR person plugging *The Erotic Review* who suggested that we do this interview (and who was probably hoping it would appear somewhere with more readers) referred to your new bit of writing for that magazine as 'a piece' in their first few emails, then finally broke down and called it a poem.
Yeah, it's poetry – I love prose poetry.

As someone who writes short fiction, how clear in your mind is the divide between a prose poem and a short story?
Really clear, actually. Though I don't really think in wholes – with a W, not just an H, because I *do* obviously think in holes with just an H! *[Laughs]* You can't really talk about this stuff without sounding pretentious.

Please try.
I tend to start with a first image, and the image will tell me what form it belongs in. The line that comes out of that will tell me it's going to work itself out as a prose poem, or as a short story. I've never got it wrong, so far. I don't think I've ever started in one form and had to switch to another.

It's funny, when I was asked to write that new poem, I struggled. I found it really hard to get back into poetry. It's the hardest of all the tasks, it's really hard to get into that headspace. It takes so much more confidence, it's so much more humiliating.

Why is poetry humiliating?
I think if you asked any poet they would say the same thing. All writing is innately embarrassing, but there's something especially humiliating about the poem. It's the more daring act, it comes with a lot of different baggage, and it can be so bad so easily…

Poetry has different ways of being intimate. Addressing the reader, for instance, and drawing attention to the page, like you do in the first poem of *Three Births* – you go from describing a photo to addressing the reader, before you say 'pleasure will continue to fold us up (we are only pieces of paper).'
To implicate the reader, or have the reader second-guessing their

implication in the poem, I think that's kinda hot. Innately hot, right? It's in a context where that 'you' can be toyed with in a way that I find interesting. It's partly because of the nature of my work. The title of that poem is 'Pick-up Truck Sex', so you know what you're starting with. My poems have terrible titles – they just say what they are!

The Guardian's reviewer called your novel Mrs S 'essentially a lengthy prose poem'. Is that a compliment or an insult?
I can't tell. Sometimes it's both. If it's *The Guardian*, I think it's both. The response to *Mrs S* is so polarised – some people can't stand it, they find that way of reading really exhausting. I thought it was a totally normal book… I thought that it wasn't weird *enough*. I just thought of it as a novel, then people started pointing out things [such as the novel's lack of speech marks] and calling it a prose poem…

Maybe it's to do with labels. If it's labelled an 'experimental novel' some people might think it's *too normal*, but it might annoy a different set of people for the opposite reason if they find it in, say, the 'Romance and Erotica' section of WHSmith.
It does on Goodreads. People on Goodreads were very bothered! [*laughs*] It throws people off. It's a bit funny for me to have it categorised as romance – I've been in a few events or panels where I've had to answer to this idea of romance as a genre.

Who writes well about sex and bodies?
A lot of Robert Glück's work does that fantastically, for example in his novel *Margery Kempe*. Harry Josephine Giles's *Them!* is so great. And I've been re-reading TS Eliot's *Four Qu-*. 🍎 **TFS**

Searing Honesty

There are few contemporary poets so alive to the liminal spaces of lived experience. Here is a bold new voice, a poet of place, identity, and history's erasures, attending with a kind of searing honesty to the intricacies and uncertainties of what it means – and doesn't mean – to be alive in the modern world. There are some fine poems here.

Here is a poetry of:

fierce intelligence
wry, clear-seeing compassion
dazzling virtuosity
luminous detail
untold stories

and devastating moments when lyrical utterance and a probing intelligence collapse the liminal spaces of lived experience. Secret histories tumble across the page like birds: 'a flurry of transient figures, / gull, goose, starling.' His is a poetry of

taut, disquieting lyricism
astonishing technical assurance
raw emotion
      (dissected with a
               wry, probing
               fierce
               razor-sharp
     intelligence)

which is at once tender and searching, timeless and, emphatically, of our time.

Hers is a poetry of sheer verbal joy, of searching, even disquieting, curiosity, and wry observations on quotidian life: by turns playful, indignant, meditative and dazzlingly intimate; radically, brilliantly unconventional in almost every way, and wonderfully self-aware. Always compelling, and often simply virtuosic, she writes with:

uncommon insight and authority
an impressive command of her craft
a ludic, streetwise sophistication
a terse delicacy that is rare in younger poets.

In this startling, uncompromising first collection, we find the steady gaze of an acute poetic eye for what is normally unseen, a rare lyrical ear for what is left unsaid. Heartbreakingly sad and laugh-out-loud funny, often in the same poem (I am thinking especially of the stand-out title poem), equally at home in

trenchant political satire
the intricacies of Japanese folklore
the farther reaches of the Berlin club scene
the back-catalogue of the Beastie Boys
the liminal spaces of lived experience

this consummately assured debut surely announces the arrival of a major new figure. Here is a book to which you will want to return again and again, each time with fresh admiration. He writes with a rollicking insouciance matched only by his dizzying, luminous clarity.

→ casual lack of conc

Riffing on scraps of modern consumerist culture, this is a poet whose hard-won intelligence and remarkable authority belie her apparent whimsicality—readers can expect poem after poem of staggering originality:

glinting with violence
timely and elegiac
        (but never sentimental)
unflinching, visceral, raw,
sassy and sexy
        (and often extremely funny)
astonishingly well crafted
at times literally breathtaking

and wonderfully alert to what it means to be alive in the world.
    A fresh new voice. 🍏 AW

Sarcastic account of the exaggerations found in bl

Apology for the foregoing

Yes, even bugbears such as 'raw' and 'breathtaking' can be right and judicious sometimes, while 'luminous', 'fierce', even 'visceral', are fine words in this context generally, only suffering, all too often, the sad fate of having bugbeardom thrust upon them. Individual elements are not presented here as necessarily objectionable.

It is in the status of the cliché that the problem resides, and since we all use clichés almost all the time – so that they are, in a sense, humanly sanctified globules of communicative communality, warmed for us by use – obviously it is indecent for anyone to deride or reject them too categorically. But just as we must decide for ourselves what is *too* categorical, so it is for everyone individually to take a view on the question of when a piece of utterance, or a whole field of utterance, has become too far dominated by cliché, or when the clichés become deadening or hollow instead of expressive.

The *pasticcio* above is not, as I see it, an attack on each of its items. It is meant as a critical indication of habitual characteristics – and, moreover, of a resultant character of habituality which sometimes seems to settle on the reviewing columns. Dead and dying metaphors, like many dead and dying things, evoke particular unease. But it is not all about metaphor and the inflation of emphatic overstatement, otherwise forgivable or expressive. Sentence structure and cadence may also be cliché.

And at what point does the prevalence of a received habit of expression, a 'mainstream' idiolect, become inconsistent with independent and diverse critical thinking? ❧ **AW**

A second piece to further explain/justify

iews

Crummy Verse

The poet and lecturer Dr Sam Riviere – author of *81 Austerities*, *Dead Souls*, *Kim Kardashian's Marriage*, etc – opens up his laptop in a small room full of undergraduates. This is not a smooth manoeuvre. The screen of Riviere's MacBook puts up some sticky resistance. It peels away from the keyboard like a shoe from the grip of bubblegum. This is only a slight exaggeration; I have seen it myself, having once been a student of Dr R.

For Riviere, a laptop holds not just data, but what a beard might for Roald Dahl's Mr Twit: pastry crumbs, streaks of old jam sandwiches, the rubble of bygone Hobnobs. Perhaps, for the writer, this is the laptop's great technological leap. In one sleek device, you have both notepad and dinnerplate.

Sam Riviere is an often-irreverent poet, one who could be seen to escape the endless mulch of 'bad internet poetry' through his commitment to process. He is not a poet overly concerned with the flakes of sausage roll under his spacebar. Evidently. Those are but found things, found crumbs, found crud. They are matter and material. He has clearly not cleaned the keyboard in a while. Perhaps he has not found a suitable method.

For – as we know from his poetry – when Riviere gathers up found material, from search engine results to Martial's epigrams, he usually first establishes a procedural constraint. In his recent collection *Conflicted Copy*, for example, he only chose words presented to him by an AI chatbot-like predictive text interface.

For Riviere, poets are always going through *processes*, it's just that we are too frequently unaware of their terms. Often, our unconscious guiding principle is to write what we think a poem *should* be. Should it have high emotional stakes? Invest in the lyric 'I'? Reject it wholly?

We are hungry for poem-writing, but it's hard to find anything new to scran. To remedy this, we sit down at our desks, guided by a peckishness that proves hard to disentangle from the material we've tasted and enjoyed before. I'm hungry for biscuits. I'm hungry for free verse and a wry laconic tone.

So, some rules and constraints: next time you're in Greggs, I compel you not to dash towards the donuts. Instead, restrict yourself to the lukewarm oven section, and select a pastry in an elaborate manner of your choosing. Eat it while you write. Be guided by the fall of crumbs, and by the act of sweeping them up. (Please, Sam, don't forget the second part.)

I've heard you can make the word TYPEWRITER entirely with the top row of keys. Maybe start there. Then, wet-wipe under the next row. Have a little nibble. See what other words you can make. 🍃 JBR

Elizabeth Bishop's need for speed

A recent survey of the automotive in modern poetry (that I've just made up) shows that tractors receive vastly more focus per stanza than motor cars. Tractors go at poet speed. They are good at moving shit around and slowing other road users down. While they favour muted colours like green and brown, they also have a lofty viewpoint. Fundamentally, they are just more poet-shaped.

'Most poets can't drive a car and the ones who do drive shouldn't,' as Don Paterson put it in 2023, voicing the popular view. There is no love lost between poets and the car industry. Manufacturers have always preferred naming conventions around stars, geography and wild animals rather than actual bards. Who wants a Ford Tennyson parked in the drive? Imagine being caught speeding in a Nissan Mishima or asleep at the lights in a Citroen Rimbaud. You are going down for a long time.

Famously, when the Ford Motor Company asked Marianne

Moore to name their new series of cars in 1955, they turned down every single one of her 43 suggestions. (Rejected options included: Anticipator, Symmechromatic, The Intelligent Whale, Utopian Turtletop, Pluma Piluma and Mongoose Civique.)

For poets, public transport wins every time. [*For more about poets on public transport, see 'A. Driver, a driver' on p. 85 – Ed*] Depending on your country of origin, you get to see the outside world whizz or grumble past without being a danger to yourself or others. You can make notes, and sneak a drink or a sandwich while listening to Einstürzende Neubauten. And, all the while, you can be as introspective as the muse demands with barely a carbon toeprint.

And yet Speed is pure sensation, and poets are not immune to its allure. Many of them (like many of us) would die for a decent thrill. Move over James Dean, Paul Newman and Steve McQueen – here comes Elizabeth Bishop. Like the three famous speed-freak actors, the poet also possessed a black MG TD sports car. Hers had red leather seats and a chrome grille. All paid for in 1953 thanks to her short story 'In the Village' appearing in *The New Yorker*. She writes to Robert Lowell about how 'It zooms up the mountains with the cut-out open' and encloses a photograph of her posing in the driving seat with her cat Tobias who looks like Bulgakov's Behemoth.

As her poem 'The Moose' indicates, no-one can fault Bishop for road awareness, nor an appreciation of the humble bus. But Bishop chose the automotive and velocity, as did a madcap John Betjeman decades earlier, throttling his open-topped Morris Cowley down the leafy lanes of the West Country. He was fined £4 for busting the 20-mph speed limit. To this day, Dorset police still look dimly upon reckless poets – as I know to my own cost. 🐝 **MF**

Our stockists

The Little Review is found on the shelves of only the very finest bookmongers. Here are a few of those charming places:

Unitom *Manchester*
Novel *Sheffield*
La Biblioteka *Sheffield*
● Heffers *Cambridge* ●
● Topping & Co *Ely* ●
Gulp Fiction *Oxford*
The Winding Stair *Dublin*
Whitechapel Gallery *London*
South London Gallery *London*
Housmans *London*
Libreria *London*
● London Review Bookshop *London* ●
John Sandoe (Books) *London*
The Gilded Acorn Bookshop *London*
Morocco Bound *London*
Lala Books *London*
Review *London*

If you know of an excellent shop that ought to be stocking The Little Review, email us at mailbox@thelittlereview.co.uk

Reviews

A blues thing, a John Donne thing

My reading of Diane Seuss's *frank: sonnets* was interrupted by a bad oyster. The illness that followed was so acute and unpleasant that in cold sweats on the bathroom floor at three in the morning I achieved a zen-like unity of body and mind – a moment of sublime and excruciating absolute presence. My reading of Diane Seuss's *frank: sonnets* was also interrupted, alongside this, by my work as a high school English teacher. I was making my way through a stack of personal essays, encountering again and again that most adolescent of grammatical missteps: the comma splice.

In Diane Seuss's *Modern Poetry*, a more recent collection than *frank*, though published on the same day in the UK, there is a poem called 'Comma'. The word 'comma' derives from the Greek for a 'piece cut off'. The poem is about contact and separation – 'never to be touched in that way. / You know what way.' – and ways a comma can change a sentence: 'Don't / narrativize, Diane. Don't narrativize Diane'. As Seuss says, 'See what a comma can do?'

'It is abominable, unquenchable by touch', begins the fifth poem in *frank*, the first of many in the book to be punctuated almost entirely by commas. 'It' is 'the need for love revolting and grand' in the eyes of 'every freak', among whose number Seuss counts Emily Dickinson. Dickinson is famous, of course, for her 'penmanship unreadable' and her dashes, which often flew low and short enough to be (couldn't they? some of them?) errant commas. She turns up later, when Seuss's father is laid in 'Dickinson's coffin', a 'box' which is elsewhere 'the exoskeleton of a book […] or poem', 'the entrapment of form', and a 'prison of paper and ink'. Seuss's sonnets are boxy things that eschew almost all formal constraint except their 14-line extent and, occasionally, quietly, the contact of a final rhyming couplet.

One of these poems is so 'unquenchable' that it needs a foldout page to contain it. Seuss writes in a single exploding sentence of casting two crackheads from her drug-addicted son's apartment 'full of dog shit', of staying 'awake' through the C-section that birthed her son, of biking as a girl through floodwater that 'must have been full of shit', and of her son who 'put his hands' on her as if intent on violence. The sensorial intensity of these memories, these abject points of contact, spills over the comma-spliced clauses to become grammatically simultaneous. They culminate in a final request: 'don't ask for my touch is what I'm saying, don't ask me to walk among the people'.

Seuss's commas are tender: an overwhelming softness between ideas, or bruises where ideas shouldn't have touched. When her teacher breaks the news of her father's death, 'tears stuck to her cheek like leeches or jewels', like a parasite, like a luxury, as if they were the same thing, and as if the hurt was itself the extravagance: 'when I have been suffering at times I could / step away from it by embracing it, a blues thing, / a John Donne thing, divest by wrestling, then sing'. Like her father cutting a hole in a table to accommodate a stovepipe, Seuss accommodates her form to 'the mind like a jackrabbit bounding, bounding' so her poems can 'respond to the absolute present' (the moment, or the gift?) of pains personal and economic and political: 'fascism in America is loud', 'The sonnet, like poverty, teaches you what you can do / without'.

I should have clocked the oysters. It was a week after Valentine's Day and they were £1. I didn't know what I could do without. The shells piled up like those personal essays piled comma upon comma, clause upon clause, each one an 'absolute present'. In the boxy form of a life, how do we touch one another, how do we cut ourselves off? By the end of *frank: sonnets*, the answers are piled in front of us: 'oyster shells gleaming silver, poetry, the only gold', ❧ **MG**

frank: sonnets by Diane Seuss (Fitzcarraldo, 2025; £12.99)

The train in Spain

Cherishing as I do memories of a double-decker Spanish train
that treated its passengers to piped light classical music, I wonder
if I harbour a naively idealist view of the European train poem.
The UK model remains chronically lumbered with Larkin-era
rolling stock, but the continental equivalent – how clean, elegant
and efficient it must be! Testing this thesis against the work of
rail fanatic Gilles Ortlieb's *The Day's Ration* returns a mixed ver-
dict. The landscape is bleak, the towns we pass through remind-
ing the narrator of the mining disasters that occurred there, but
the writing goes like this:

> Strange sulphurous-tinted lichen
> invades the embankments under the untroubled
> blue sky, still criss-crossed with the disaffected
> blast-pipes of the furnaces; further off

the rail-forging factory, having done so much
work unrusting can now, in peace at last
where the country has resumed, rust over.

All that post-industrial decline sits easily alongside the window-seat botanism, resisting programmatic grimness and twee pastoral alike. Romer and McGuinness are right, in their afterword, to stress Ortlieb's precision and ability to do justice to the duality of staying and going simultaneously, finding stillness in the moving train, and transition in the temporary halts of his hotels. His is a divided self, inspecting a frontier that is 'two hundred metres / and ten years ago', forever 'hesitating between me and me'. Rail journeys are pre-determined in ways that road trips aren't, yet the force of the unknown is undimmed ('the perfect geometry of steel threads: two pairs of rails / stretching towards the unknown corners of the soul'). Ortlieb is the 'eternal last passenger', running to make his connection, 'becoming that someone else / – why bother travelling otherwise? – / already awaiting your arrival', and *The Day's Ration* is one of the best books of poetry in translation published in recent years. ❧ **DW**

The Day's Ration: Selected Poems by Gilles Ortlieb, trs Stephen Romer and Patrick McGuinness (Arc Publications, 2023; £8.99)

Bull Island

Pádraig Ó Tuama presents the podcast *Poetry Unbound*. Out of that podcast, an anthology emerged: *Poetry Unbound: 50 Poems to Open your World* (Canongate, 2022). Note the title. Poetry is closed to you, and so is your world. But here comes Ó Tuama, a sort of universal dilator who opens everything up.

Gush is often the consequence. Here's a testimonial, quoted on his website: 'Pádraig Ó Tuama is an extraordinary person, whose influence extends quietly and gracefully across the world. His poetry bears these same qualities and brings him close. It is a gift to us all.'

Ó Tuama's background is in liberal and post-secular theology. From 2014-2019, he led the peace-promoting Corymeela Community in Northern Ireland. Such organisations do wonderful work. But they are a blanket over barbed wire; the thinking that emerges will quite deliberately not be sharp. When Ó Tuama talks about spiritual matters, this is what he sounds like:

> To greet sorrow today does not mean that sorrow will be there tomorrow. Happiness comes too, and grief, and tiredness, disappointment, surprise and energy. Chaos and fulfilment will be named as well as delight and despair. This is the truth of being here, wherever here is today. It may not be permanent but it is here. I will probably leave here, and I will probably return. To deny here is to harrow the heart. Hello to here.

For people exhausted by suffering, by long and bitter conflict and division, this sort of thinking and writing is refreshing and necessary. Its USP is its softness, its indulgence: it's gush. But if it works in one place, that doesn't mean it works everywhere. Muck helps the crops grow, but you don't want it extending quietly and gracefully across the world.

Kitchen Hymns, Ó Tuama's latest collection, shows the danger. In attempting to move further from tatty old theology towards the prestige of literature (Ó Tuama no longer describes himself as believing in God) he can't seem to leave behind theology's verbosity and woolliness. It often dribbles into bathos:

> I bless myself in the name
> of the deer and ox,
> the heron and the hare,
> evangelists of land and wood
> and air. The fox as well, that red
> predator of chickens, prey of cars.

The writing can come across as pleased with itself; a prose poem made of fan-mail from a homophobic fan ('I love your writing, even though you're a homosexual') is a case in point. Elsewhere, Ó Tuama quotes Rumi approvingly – 'If anyone asks: "How did Jesus raise the dead?" kiss me on the lips, say: like this!'– and clearly aspires in his own work to that level of mystic twaddle:

I asked the songthrush about the soul
and it sang until a gate to hell opened.
I asked the mountain what mattered.
It said nothing.

But in case he sounds too naïve, Ó Tuama also wants us to know he can write about 'the quantum unconscious' and 'psychoneuroimmunology'. This seems to backfire when 'equiprimordality' appears – the word is equiprimordiality.

Most poets want to appear on podcasts – and would give their eye-teeth for inclusion in a Canongate anthology – so Ó Tuama's projects will have put him in touch with many peers. Given this, it's a shame that it seems none of the excellent poets mentioned in his acknowledgements gave him proper feedback on his poems. At the heart of this book is an autobiographical sequence of 13 poems, each one titled with the question 'Do you believe in God?'. Here's one:

At twenty-three I walked in the dark
to Bull Island's stretch of beach.
I stood beneath the statue of the
Virgin Mary. Star of the Sea.
I took off all my clothes and shouted

I am lonely at the water.

It was the middle of the night.
There was the smell of oil
and rotting seaweed,
the glow of factories,
smoke catching all the light
from Dublin city.

There's obvious absurdity here: Bull Island indeed. To the cry '*I am lonely*' the reader shouts back 'I'm not surprised'. But it's quite an achievement to get so much repetition and redundancy into such a short poem. Get your red pen out and play along at home. 'It was the middle of the night' and 'in the dark'? Have one but not both. A stretch of beach is just a beach. Statue? OK, so this is not the woman herself we're talking about – good to know.

Accentuating the poet's loneliness with four consecutive 'I's would be neatly done, if it wasn't followed by the thudding obviousness of that explicit statement ('*I am lonely*'). Oil, seaweed and factories can all be invoked without the verbal run-up. The image of 'smoke catching all the light' from the city sounds fine but means little. Catching? *All* the light? And we end at Dublin city, to which the only response is 'oh that Dublin'.

The best poem here is the nastiest. 'Eat This Bread' gives a good description of the hunger of baby birds in the nest, satirising religious longing with self-disgust:

You are unceasing. A baby. A bomb.
You are all hunger, no flight or song.

The way the light shines through the
tissue of your beak. Your eyes wide.
Round. The raw need, the pink demand
of you. I can't stand you.

Suddenly, with negativity comes a sharpness that trims all fat from the poem – it has real muscle. There's a sense behind the poem of deep pain and anger restrained and focused in simple, accurate description. It just might be that poetry bound, poetry closed, poetry where the gushing flood is channeled to a jet, is the real deal. ❧ **GR**

Kitchen Hymns by Pádraig Ó Tuama (Cheerio, 2025; £12)

Request

Now it's our turn to approach the table
the Edinburgh Book Festival has installed you at,
pen in hand when not the tumbler, my brother
asks you about knowing Kavanagh.
Patrick Kavanagh, you say, was a sweet and crude man:
he wrote about fifteen poems that are – immortal.
It's possible that you wrote one, one only.
That's all we can reasonably ask.

🍎 HC

Brutal.

Did HC and brother actually meet Longley in Edinburgh

Ash Keys: New and Selected Poems by Michael Longley
(*Jonathan Cape, 2024; £16*)

Essential gaudiness

inventing new words

With its hot pink cover and neologising title, Ange Mlinko's *Foxglovewise* is no wallflower. An epigraph, from Louise Glück's 'Matins', contrasts staid hawthorn with the 'inconsistent' foxglove, and, as in Mlinko's title poem, in which she 'stray[s] off the map', we're meant to plump for the latter. Nobody wants to take the path *more* travelled.

Still, it seems odd for Mlinko to champion the unruly. The poet and critic is known as a formalist, committed to metre and rhyme, and for all that her seventh collection approves errancy, it doesn't deviate from her usual methods. Unlike, say, those of her Florida-poet predecessor Elizabeth Bishop, Mlinko's formal schemes rarely go under the radar. She's fond of a variant of terza rima in which the rhymes match line-for-line across stanzas – ABC, ABC – like a particularly emphatic waltz. She rhymes with Byronic brio: 'in my mind's eye' couples with 'cumulonimbi'.

State or quality of being in error

daring than advertised

Mlinko's unabashed delight in language is refreshing, when it isn't a little tiring. In 'To My Hummingbird', she asks: 'Am I a sommelier / to provide miniscule / kraters for proboscises?' Mixing words of disparate pedigrees isn't invariably a bad idea – I like Wallace Stevens and his 'jovial hullabaloo' – but here, the French 'sommelier' pouring from ancient Greek 'kraters' is a bit much. Stevens, in fact, looms over much of the book, from its florid Floridian vistas to its delight in what he called the 'essential gaudiness of poetry'. One poem nicks a line from his 'Sea Surface Full of Clouds', while the collection's opener, about Maria Callas, at times edges past homage into impersonation: 'so that she moved and sang in fictive stanzas'; 'and the modal melodies strike our ear as from the East'.

Like Stevens, though, Mlinko is at her best when she gives the big words room to breathe, setting them off against a sparser, clearer diction. In 'Adult Ballet', 'suspension of disbelief / gives rise to a shaky arabesque'. The lower register makes the last word feel earned – a quality of a piece with the poem's interest in patient practice: 'One returns, to forms of humility', it begins. I love the ending of 'The Rain Trees', its monosyllables splatting like fat drops: 'Can rain trees slake a parti pris / for elegy, for rain's right clink, / and claim spring's shade?' These lines have the shimmer of music, rather than a lexicographical glint.

So *Foxglovewise* is an uneven collection. A long poem (or possibly an unnumbered sonnet sequence), 'Chekhov in the Gulf of Mexico', is a masterpiece of tempo and pitch. 'A man, with his actress companion, appears. / The palms start up like a band in a sudden breeze': Mlinko, risking the prosaic, achieves a cinematic sweep and focus. But in the collection's next poem, 'The Mechanicals', this social-realist mode feels weirdly stilted. A hairdresser's gossip doesn't sound like a real person: 'Airbags use a powder that leaves burns / when they're deployed.' The two sides of Mlinko's art – her extraordinary ear for language, and her wry, amused perceptiveness of self and world alike – don't always come together. (Sometimes they even seem incompatible.) But when they do fuse, the book glows. 🐛 **BP**

Foxglovewise by Ange Mlinko (Faber, 2025; £12.99)

Great summation of a mixed bag.

...le/diction of prose instead of poetry; ...king originality (!)

3.62 packets of crisps

Sad! Ne[...]
to me

To read the subtitle: *An Affordable Anthology of Contemporary Poetry*. To read the price: £3.99.

To pick up a copy 20 minutes after seeing an Instagram announcement that the Arts Council has decided to defund Broken Sleep because they're broke.

To pick up a bag of Walkers Salt & Vinegar and do some quick arithmetic.

To open at the opening line of *Opening Line*: 'finally! you've come to visit' and to consider visit as poem.[1] Here we are. How long shall we stay. To consider a small book as a door. ♡

An opening line – hello.

Or a line that is itself open – a line that is not quite open but will take you if you let it.

Line – boundary, border, weather front, pathway on a map. To let is also to go.

To be open to all weather: 'Last night I fell into the airspace / over Gaza',[2] Portobello Rugby Football Club.[3] To notice pressures coming in and high winds. To squeeze in a world of small things.

To notice no agenda to the crisps. Some big some small some needing crunch and some melting on tongue: 'None of us / knows how to transcend tenderness yet.'[4]

To put down. To let breathe. To follow the directions printed at the back of every Broken Sleep book: LAY OUT YOUR UNREST, followed by five blank pages. Because 'something out of broken sleep will land / there.'[5] There: empty shelf, corner of a mind opening with satisfying crinkle.

To read it all again in June, 'And see I'm calling now, whether or not / this is now or in time.'[6]

To consider small things as lasting. To consider fragile beginnings. To hope for more – 🐰 JW

> Open-ended. Not finished?

Opening Line: An Affordable Anthology of Contemporary Poetry, ed Aaron Kent (Broken Sleep Books, 2025, £3.99)

[1] 'Sweet, sweet' by Anthony Vahni Capildeo
[2] 'Cushioned' by Luke Lankester
[3] 'Glimpsed Glory: Portobello Rugby Football Club' by Michael Pederson
[4] 'Teeth' by Hannah Copley
[5] 'Smaller than the Radius of the Planet' by JH Prynne
[6] 'In June' by Will Harris ✳

Boo!

Alex Mazey has invented a new kind of imagism in *Ghost Lives: Cursed Edition*. The lyric poems that comprise about a third of the book are of the traditional variety; they deal frequently in bold colours (trees 'orange against // an otherwise green prevalence', 'board of yellow wood', 'a red sun, and a red dress', 'this glass with blue and pink'). They balance strange objects atop one another as they relate moody scenes through a jazzy haze. They're attentive to light ('the backlit forest', 'Your bedroom light's distance', 'The warm-cold light') but are more likely to deploy symbols of light-against-blackness: vending machines, glow sticks, pachinko and arcade machines, exit signs, lighthouses, karaoke bars. In the same vein, their dark edges come rimed with sugar: iced tea, fruit mochi, 7-UP, incense, pop rocks, cherry blossom, 'sweet oranges' and so on. It's poetry collection as Tokyo nightclub.

The rest of the book, more startlingly, is made up of Unicode poems – that is, text art in mostly monospace font. Here's a simple example:

ﾉ o_o)

　　ﾉ o_o)

('Ghost Is Haunted by a Much Larger and Scarier Ghost')

These poems depart from the better-known examples of concrete and calligraphic poetry by being unreadable except as images – they're 95% punctuation mark. But they're also a lot more straightforward than what lurks on the unrulier side of visual poetry; all are miniature portraits of the above character, Ghost, at the midpoint of some kind of errand, excursion or chain of events. 'Ghost Sees a Cat', 'Ghost Visits a Hotel Sauna at 8am', 'Ghost Interprets a Road Sign as a Message From the Universe'.

The normally mute Ghost is adorable even when doing ghosty things, and the scenarios are as funny as they are bleak. Where they find their footing as poems is in unexpected, provocative juxtapositions. 'Ghost Passes Through a Disused Train Yard' is followed immediately by 'Ghost Is Hit by a Train In Use'. It looks like the same train. Was the train yard not disused at all? Did Ghost glitch? Is he dead? Is he suddenly tangible?

Similarly, and more slyly, 'Ghost Sees a Mushroom Cloud on the Horizon' comes one page before 'Ghost Uses a Magic Eight Ball'. What does the eight ball say? 'Outlook not so good'. 'Ghost is Sent to the Gulag' follows on the heels of 'Ghost Possesses a Fruit Machine'. 'Ghost Makes It Rain' (in which Ghost swings round a stripper pole as dollar bills are thrown into the air) precedes 'Ghost Stands in the Rain' (in which Ghost… stands in the rain). The details in the images are also delightfully morbid: 'PILLS + PILLS + PILLS +' reads a sign for a pharmacy.

At the time of writing the book hasn't found its way onto any prize shortlists. I'm sure that's partly because it's comfortably in touch with its pop culture influences in a way that verges on heretical. There remains an expectation that poetry adopt an attitude of either rarefaction or commonplaceness – go high or go low. When it comes to so much of the contemporary media kaleido-scape, a poem may namedrop, appropriate or subvert with a gleam in its eye, but must never marry into the family.

Mazey gleefully references video games ('Ghost Considers Playing Level II', 'Ghost in the Style of a Survival Horror Minimap') but more than that, his timbre is three parts *Undertale* to two parts e. e. cummings. Creepypasta, lo-fi beats and seinen manga are written into *Ghost Lives'* DNA, mingling with William Carlos Williams and Anne Carson. Even the title, with its colon and claim to being an 'edition', is an impish nod to recuts, remasters and DLCs (downloadable content). As such, it stands on a threshold, opening a doorway where there was previously a canyon – a shame that few are likely to take the opportunity to cross. ❦ JS

Ghost Lives: Cursed Edition by Alex Mazey
(Bad Betty Press, 2024; £10.99)

A hot tip,
just 167 years late

Word of mouth is what every marketeer wants. It's what sells dog food, and varifocal glasses, and even, occasionally, books.

For poetry, word of mouth does more than that. It's how I know what I'm enjoying. The poetry that delights me is the poetry that insists on becoming words in my mouth, words on my tongue and my lips, twice over. The first time is when I read a poem and need to speak it aloud, to make it fill up a room as it fills up a page. To hear the consonants click and the sibilants hiss and the rhymes chime or miss. And the second is when I need to talk about them, to tell other people about this poem, this poet, this experience of reading.

Lately, I've told my cousin in New Zealand about David Jones's *In Parenthesis*: she said she was 'almost tempted to read it'. I've told my optician about Nia Broomhill's poem 'Varifocals': he asked me to send him a copy to frame on the wall. The latest poem that I've vocalised, voiced, been vociferous about, is Arthur Hugh Clough's verse novel *Amours de Voyage*. This is not a new poem – it was published in 1858 – but there's no reason only to review new poetry. [*This sets a dangerous precedent; let's not pull at that thread – Ed.*] It was republished by Persephone Press a few years ago, so you can buy it with a sleek grey cover and patterned bookmark.

Amours de Voyage is set in Italy during the Roman Revolution of 1848, as a group of English tourists are disturbed to find that History is not confined to the past. In fact, History is going on all around them. Claude, our hero, is a smug young man on a gap year, ready to tell his friends how much Rome disappoints his elevated tastes. It's only when there's no milk for his cafe latte that he realises that the city is under siege by the French army. Meanwhile, the Trevellyn sisters are observing and judging Claude.

The verse novel is told in a series of letters from the different characters, and in hexameters throughout. The form seems to have sprung from Claude's clever but limited mind: shaped by his public school education in the classics, Claude insists on slotting Rome as it is into the template he was given. Claude, when we first meet him, has an ability to pontificate on almost any subject – religion, history, art, philosophy, etc, etc – with a wonderful condescension.

> What do I think of the Forum? An archway and two or
>   three pillars.
> Well, but St. Peter's? Alas, Bernini has filled it with
>   sculpture!
> No one can cavil, I grant, at the size of the great
>   Coliseum…

'Brickwork I found thee, and marble I left thee!' their
   Emperor vaunted
'Marble I thought thee, and brickwork I find thee!' the
   Tourist may answer.

Georgina Trevellyn is interested purely in the social life the other
English travellers might provide. She writes in a letter:

Rome is a wonderful place, but Mary shall tell you about it;
Not very gay, however; the English are mostly at Naples;
There are the A.'s, we hear, and most of the W. party.
George, however, is come; did I tell you about his
   mustachios?

But our English tourists are about to learn something more of
life. When Claude finds himself on the edge of a lynch-mob, the
professional sightseer unable to see what is happening, his slick
lines give way to hesitation:

But a man was killed, I am told, in a place where I saw
Something; a man was killed, I am told, and I saw
   something.

Amours de Voyage begins to ask what it means to be 'told' about
the world, what it means to 'see' a place, and what 'something'
might mean. In these two lines, repetition and the line break
bring the guidebook's endless clarity into question.

There's a real pleasure in seeing what Clough can do with a
hexameter, and how he can coax it into the many different voices
of his narrators. Clough also takes delight in subverting narra-

tive expectations, and the ending of this tale of romance amid revolution is comically flat. But it's worth noting that the poem was based on his own experiences of being in Rome under siege.

The mockery of the tourists, who can see only what their guidebook has told them to see, conveys a genuine warning. And it's one that applies as much today as it did to the young intellectuals of the smug 1850s. We may not be using *Murray's Handbook for Travellers* today, and Instagram has replaced the letter to friends, but our society has certainly retained the desire to experience and report the world only through a series of pre-packaged opinions. ❦ **HT**

Amours de Voyage by Arthur Hugh Clough
(Persephone Press, 2009; £17)

'Have I even talked about her butt yet?'

Peter Hughes's *Cavalcanty* (2017) is one of the best books I've ever been sent for review. So good is it that I lent it to an acquaintance, and two years on am still trying to get it back. I therefore have to quote it from memory, but lines like 'My soul has pressed its nose against the glass / in search of likes and messages from you' lodge pretty inextricably in the brain. It made Cavalcanti's Italian eroto-metaphysical angst our own, somehow knocking out seven hundred years of cultural distance; it fused social media with *dolce stil novo*, producing stuff like this:

This autumn I Guido Cavalcanti
legendary co-founder of the Dolce
& Gabbana mode of filling colour
supplements & academic footnotes
turn my back on all the peer reviewing

But of course you can't turn your back on the peer reviewing, and Hughes now opens himself up to it again with *Jack Lentini & the Pirate Queen*, 23 versions of poems by another 13th-century writer: Giacomo da Lentini, the Sicilian notary accused of inventing the sonnet. The tone is still brattishly postmodern –

> the jury's still out as to whether
> or to what extent a modern English line
> or vintage Sicilian smoothied into Tuscan
> could register the glances sweat & yearn

– and yes, I too initially read that as 'smoothed'. And Hughes still shows a gift for trashification that can implicate poetry – that of Lentini and Elizabeth Barrett Browning, in this case – with the glitz of consumerism:

> Let me count the ways
> she is not like a diamond
> ruby or saxophone solo
> or ham on a plinth
> or the latest Milanese collections

The above quotation is typical of these poems' jerky arrhythmia. Despite their non-punctuation, very few of *Cavalcanty*'s sonnets strayed from ten-syllable lines, creating a breathless pulse that flirted with pentameter and used the line break as a semantic weapon. Sadly, *Jack Lentini & the Pirate Queen* is too choppy to spool up the same kind of momentum:

> we're opening a little jar
> of last night's light and capers
> a hint of island flugelhorn
> drifts through certain alleys
> from the principle [*sic*] piazza
> she turns to me
> adjusts my mouth and stars

Not only did the sonnets in *Cavalcanty* and *Quite Frankly* (Hughes's rendition of Petrarch) actually look like sonnets; at their best, they made you experience a sort of erotic asphyxiation. Thematically, *Jack Lentini* aspires to a similar sly lubriciousness – 'I need to scooch & swivel to address / the subject properly / O my America! My newfoundland'. But then the poem becomes lazily crass: 'have I even talked about her butt yet / probably not – you would have remembered'.

Then again, the weird 'pirate queen' thread in this pamphlet does smack of teenage fantasy: one suspects that Hughes just saw the chance for some nautical puns, like 'of course I adore her unregistered sloop / her informal crew and booty'. He might have spared himself 'her parrots of the Caribbean', but the reader has already realised that the book is less 'Jack' Lentini than Jack Sparrow. 🌿 **HC**

Jack Lentini & the Pirate Queen by Peter Hughes
(Knives Forks & Spoons Press, 2024; £7)

A Corker

Urban Irish poetry written in the 1970s and not about Dublin or Belfast was not the most abundant of commodities. Yet the map is not entirely bare: Eiléan Ní Chuilleanáin's *Cork* (1977) is a classic of the genre, now repackaged with artwork by Brian Lalor for a welcome reissue.

Irish writing is often topographically hyperspecific, yet here 'We could be in any city.' Two decades before Ní Chuilleanáin's birth, Cork had been a major theatre of the Irish revolutionary period, and the stamp of history mixes unobtrusively with the natural depradations of flooding:

> Shopfronts now reduced to a man's height,
> The mark of fire and water
> Still stamped black on paint and plaster.

Its mix of old and new imbues the dead in post-independence Ireland with a curiously vital quality:

> In the graveyards of the city, wells
> of arrested sound,
> the tombstones are swaying like a house of cards.

The lyric 'I' at large in these locales is vague and mysterious, its intimate adventures already auditioning for the allegorical transformation of a statue:

> We turn away from each other,
> Our shoulders are smooth as the plaster veils of statues
> That are turning their backs in the windows and doors.

Cork is a fascinating early instalment in a body of work that, half a century later, has grown to be among the most rewarding in modern poetry. 🌑 **DW**

Cork by Eiléan Ní Chuilleanáin (Gallery Press, 2024; €25).

Zero style

Not everyone was pleased with Chinua Achebe's *Things Fall Apart* on its publication in 1958. 'An African who thinks and feels in his own language must write in that language,' wrote Obi Wali. Instead Achebe had chosen a drily bureaucratic English, almost as though the fictional author of the colonial report mentioned in the novel ('The Pacification of the Primitive Tribes of the Lower Niger') were Achebe himself. Born of a kind of mimetic complicity, as Justin Quinn shows in his *Literature in the Age of Lingua Franca English*, Achebe's veneer of bland neutrality nevertheless carries great critical force.

Today, the Achebe-Wali dichotomy remains, but in somewhat modified form. The global market craves marketable singularity, but this will often come in the form of what Quinn terms the 'zero style' – a form of global English whose language has been 'globalized, flattened, bleached, homogenized', and far from the crisp elegance of *Things Fall Apart*.

Turning to poetry, Quinn discusses Claudia Rankine's *Citizen*. For all that volume's discussion of language as a theatre of conflict, Quinn notes that it too is written in global Standard English; Rankine embraces the zero style that will allow her work to become 'globally legible'. This manoeuvre may seem ironic, but 'Rankine is beyond irony'. Terrance Hayes, by contrast, handles African-American Vernacular English (AAVE) more directly in *Sonnets for My Past and Future Assassin*, while shuttling back and forth between that AAVE and Standard English, staging a matrix of interactions that – to Quinn – nonetheless still remain squarely within the zero style paradigm.

The zero style is not a phenomenon to be merely condemned or applauded, but understood – a kind of linguistic event horizon of our times. *Literature in the Age of Lingua Franca English: The Zero Style* is a provocative book, and some will be as irked by it as Obi Wali was by Achebe. But do our objections and exceptions do anything more than prove the zero style rule? Och, I hae ma doots, as they say in my local idiolect. 🐛 **DW**

Literature in the Age of Lingua Franca English: The Zero Style by *Justin Quin* (Routledge, 2024; £36.99)

Daffodils in the waste land

From the first poem in *The New Herbal*, 'The Romance of the Rose (redux)', Fran Lock states her intention to wrest control of the floral from the formal masters, and respond to the classics with freshness and fury. A rose by any other name becomes a protest against capitalism ('a rose unfolding, like the meagre thrill of salary'), a call-out of male violence ('a stalker's wilting tantrum') and a call to arms ('a poem in which rose is the organising pronoun'). 'Daffodils' are 'hardy stragglers / between wastelands' which remind us 'we are dying. we are all / dying, but they did not get / the memo.' Nature is political, juxtaposed with 'industrial zones, border patrols, assembly lines', in 'Blue Hydrangea in mouth', whose epigraph tells us 'men in the 1800s used to send hydrangeas to women who rejected them, accusing them of frigidity…' This pamphlet reminds us beauty is not neutral; we must reflect on who gets to nurture it, wield it, or enjoy it. ❧ **DF**

The New Herbal by Fran Lock (Blueprint, 2024; £7)

A Muldoonian
virgin writes

Before reading *Joy in Service on Rue Tagore*, I had only come across Paul Muldoon as a form of insult to myself; editor after editor (comprising two total) recommended I read the Northern Irish trickster as a means of tempering what I can only interpret as a total joylessness they found in my own verse. One hundred and twenty-two pages later, I am beginning to tentatively admit Muldoon's puzzling, lilted light.

There is a sustained opposition in the spine of this collection (and, I'm told again by wincing editors, across Muldoon's *oeuvre*) between pressing, important content and ludic form. The repetition of dire themes which Samuel Beckett's verse so embodies, and the synthasthetic symbol-sound-world of Wallace Stevens. This is at it's best; Muldoon is certainly a master of parallelism, and those in poems like 'Nativity 2020', 'The Riders', 'When the Italians' and 'Near Izium' (the last dedicated to Andrey Kurkov, and reflecting on the war in Ukraine) become urgent rhythms of politic and historic disruption. The repetitions are here additive and grave. Each verse of 'The Riders' – a lyric written by Muldoon to be sung by the rock group Rogue Oliphant – ends with the same four lines:

And those of us who've ridden the white horse
In our own expeditionary force
Now weep that history must run its course
Now weep that history must run its course

Elsewhere, however, I struggle to find any purchase at all on poems like 'Horse Carpaccio', Muldoon's translation of Neruda's 'Ode to the Artichoke', or 'The Belfast Pogrom: Some Observations', where historical testimony of injustice risks being pacified into 'quite bittersweet / memories'. There's a danger at the heart of this style; I, as the reader, share with one of Muldoon's speakers a concern that the poetry is here 'less because of some profound unrest / than my fascination with the Cree'. That is, that the imposition of strange references and cultural artefacts from the author's idiosyncratic collection of interests overwhelms, and draws strength away from, the poem itself. This is a matter of personal taste, but when I encounter poems like 'At the Grave of Chang and Eng', about the 19th-century conjoined twins ('Chang and Eng are still dancing cheek to cheek // but to Nile Rodgers and Chic's "Le Freak"'), I simply don't know what they are for or what to do with them. Their oddities and details are a blank page, their whimsical rhythms received by me as muzak rather than utterance.

It's interesting that the most withheld sequences from this collection are among the most memorable – the title poem and 'The Wheel Invents the Road' have a touching vulnerability to them, which comes out from hiding behind the otherwise near-relentless ear-seduction. Lines like 'You made me what I am. / The wheel invents the road' prove that Muldoon can sustain ambiguity with restraint, and without overwhelming the reader with reference. I wonder how far he has allowed himself to tread the road of sincerity before sidestepping into soundplay, and what impulses stop him from going further.

There are long poems in *Joy in Service* ('Artichokes and Truffles', 'The Castle of Perserverance') which are likely a reader's ultimate litmus test: is this poetry really sufficient; to be taken along, in this current of amusement, through the quiddities and contradictions of history? All in all, for me at least, the paper just about blots through. I have to admit (however begrudgingly) that Muldoon's style is one he is in total command of, and one difficult to reproduce. If this level of technical artistry appeals, readers will find in *Joy in Service on Rue Tagore* a deft and eclectic collection of poems. 🌱 **WS**

*Joy in Service on Rue Tagore by Paul Muldoon
(Faber, 2024; £14.99, paperback £12.99)*

Dada data

I read somewhere that art cannot in itself be beautiful: the world is so full of beauty that art is the place of respite from it. Joanna Fuhrman's refreshing *Data Mind* (2024) takes seriously the idea of poetry as respite, offering a series of prose poems that concentrate really hard on the distractedness of life on (and life in) the internet.

Fuhrman's recent article for *Heavy Feather Review* on how poetry anticipated the internet includes an email she received from the writer William Lessard: 'There are poets like John Ashbery for whom the internet seems to have been invented who probably never sent an email'. Fuhrman's style is akin to Ashbery's sweeping comic scope. But while his poetry anticipated the algorithmically collaged surrealism of online life, hers is born out of her relationship with it: 'I thought poetry was a way to get lost like the internet', she writes in 'The Internet Is Not The City'.

And the city is an image which pervades *Data Mind*: 'My love of the internet was like my love of the city. In each, I wandered underground, smelling of pomegranates and hemorrhoid cream'. Fuhrman is the Frank O'Hara of internet back-streets, a flâneuse of obscure blogs ('I posted to a forum a question about the effects of perimenopause, and when the answers came back, I trembled in their presence') and corridors of data streams. She takes the internet as the texture of her poetry, where images collide as randomly as though pushed by an algorithm:

> She's [...] leading glow-up tutorials for itinerant mushroom clouds, gaining a following for her ASMR-inspired parenting technique, redecorating her mudroom using only syringes from defunded needle exchange programs.

The formal disjunctiveness of *Data Mind* is strangely smoothed in places, however, meditating on the way attention has been restructured around the random, comic clash of inconceivably weird images. Surrealism poured into the everyday. Data Mind can come to feel like a symptom of internet life rather than an objective attempt to describe it, particularly in lines like 'static replaces your arthritic knee', and 'the waterfalls in the cave of your mouth are now error messages'.

These are not pessimistic poems, but they probe at the question of how we can form meaningful relationships in a world that has been totally restructured by the digital. Cause and effect become jumbled as though caught in the maelstrom of discrete bits of information: 'Why don't trees fall apart when you cry?' Fuhrman is both sympathetic to the connections the internet brings between people, in the interconnected web of things that lays down the formal basis of the collection, and wary of the collapse of experience it might bring: 'I wanted everyone to feel the way my teeth vibrated', as the first poem here opens.

Data Mind thinks smartly about how poetry might interact with a language that seems its skittish opposite, avoiding the slapdash co-opting of banal internet-speak you can find almost anywhere, whilst also refusing to shy away from how language and experience have been transformed by the internet. She adopts its rhythms, revels in its Dadaist collages, but probes at its contours, its fissures, and sees how much it might be reduced to binary. ❦ **HG**

Data Mind by Joanna Fuhrman (Northwestern University Press, 2024; £17.95)

Eyes as wide as Woolf's

Lyn Hejinian (1941-2024) added back in all the context left out of her time. Her writing was no more about the self as such than Virginia Woolf's; rather, like Woolf before her, she was the widest eye of all her generation. Her death is a great loss. So, too, is a lack of a proper multi-volume Collected Works. As an opening salvo, we have *The Proposition: Uncollected Early Poems 1963-1983.* A distinguished scholarly publication, it's expensive, for the completist as an archive visit would be, and not a useful introduction. These are early bitty pieces. They are interesting because they say where they were first published, laggards of the previous avant-garde generation about to go on the scrapheap. Her experimental 'L=A=N=G=U=A=G=E Poetry' movement still needs to be sold, and the poems here are on the fault lines. If you're already a convert though, they're filler.

It's very hard to quote one in this review, and anyway Hejinian's strength is in long-form work (for which I recommend cheap purchase of the PDF of *The Cell*, or *My Life*, from the Green Integer website). There are useful snippets in the critics section at the back: Lytle Shaw laying out some of the conceptual schema, Jacob Edmond with good anecdotes about Hejinian's connections with living Russian writers. But by and large too-big claims are made for ideas of avoiding the self. Hejinian's own work asks more interesting philosophical questions, is wonderfully inclusive of all the things edited out, and she is a fine erotic love poet. Her skill is to use a term, and then make us aware of how provisional it is, in order to play with life as much as terminology. This early work also includes journeyman pieces in concrete poetry that only inform the later riches. But this short poem may take some reader's fancy, even without further reading:

May *(for Larry)*

love enough to say
to say
look out, over
four for ours

maybe May be loud

'enough'

and both enough too.   ❧ IL

The Proposition: Uncollected Early Poems 1963-1983
by Lyn Hejinian (Edinburgh University Press, 2024; £95)

Dulce et decorum

Every schoolchild knows Wilfred Owen's 'Dulce et Decorum Est', if not the Horace poem (*Odes* 3.2) from which Owen borrowed his Latin title. The First World War poets are often taught in schools on the assumption that their work is easy – but a new book from OUP, *Greek and Roman Antiquity in First World War Poetry: Making Connections*, challenges the idea that their work is in any way simple, by providing detailed commentaries on classical interactions in the war poetry of Rupert Brooke, Charles Sorley, Isaac Rosenberg and Wilfred Owen. The first two attended elite public schools, where classics was the mainstay of the curriculum, whereas Rosenberg and Owen largely had to find their own way to the classics, and the volume is alert to important differences in class and education.

The commentary's fine-grained analysis unpacks these poems' engagements with Homer, Horace and Virgil; indeed, Elizabeth Vandiver, the author of the excellent *Stand in the Trench, Achilles: Classical Receptions in British Poetry of the Great War* (2010), notes in her chapter on Owen that the commentary format forced her to reconsider her previous argument that he had probably not actually read Horace.

The book also explores how these poems shape our reading of classical texts (as readers are now likely to encounter Owen before Horace), and is sensitive throughout not just to the language of the poems themselves, but also to thorny issues such as class, race, gender, and anti-war sentiment. Chapters considering non-classical influences are particularly informative on Biblical models – which are perhaps as opaque as classical ones to the majority of readers nowadays.

While its scope may seem narrow, this study aims for a wider perspective by reflecting on how later poets such as Michael Longley and Carol Ann Duffy have responded to the treatment of the classics in First World War poets' work. Poets have been writing about the pity of war for thousands of years; this volume's analysis of the complex, often classical, richness of the verses of these soldier-poets who fought and died in the First World War goes a long way towards showing why such poetry is today considered synonymous with 'war poetry'. ❦ JI

Greek and Roman Antiquity in First World War Poetry: Making Connections, by Lorna Hardwick, Stephen Harrison, and Elizabeth Vandiver (OUP, 2024; £20)

Sweet nothings

John Phillips was born in Cornwall and now lives in the hills of central Slovenia, which is a perfect geographical parallel to his distance as a poet from the current UK poetry scene. Much of his new collection *Language Being Time* consists of brief, unpunctuated poems like the four lines of 'Given':

> the shape of
> the unseen
>
> > in the shape of
> > the seen

That's it! Actually, this is a good definition of the trajectory of a lot of poetry writing. But while most of us focus on the second couplet's 'seen', Phillips is rigorous in his emphasis on what remains 'unseen' and the book's unpunctuated and ambiguous title suggests his three major concerns.

Phillips's brevity is a breath of fresh air, as is his attention to each word's placement on the white of the page. 'After Creeley' suggests something of where he's coming from. Language is most often treated in these pages as a kind of vacation from silence which is the (more) real thing. 'Unfinished' deploys synaesthesia to suggest this: 'Each time I say a word / I hear a rustling at the edge / of light'. The preceding untitled poem says it in a different mode:

Of this
silence

I can
tell you

nothing
it can't

say for
itself

That's it (again)! The cryptic quality is only superficial, in the same way that the great Chinese classic poems of the Daodejing tease us while introducing really important themes which deepen on reflection. As for Being (the sense of our own existence), these untitled four lines do a lot of heavy lifting:

Thinking wonders
what it is

to be unthought
and still there

Two sections of about 50 such poems frame a longer sequence called 'The Creation of Beauty' which seems to have a contemporary war in mind but slips from desire to memory, from landscape to the conversation of lovers. In this sequence, dedicated to the Palestinian poet Mahmoud Darwish and the Israeli poet Yehuda Amichai, Phillips manages to say something coherent (and often beautiful) about the nightmare that is Gaza:

And as if nothing
has happened,

war still pretends
to be peace

Admirable as this sequence is, it's Phillips's poems on language, being and time that offer sustenance of a timeless quality. ❧ MC

Language Being Time by John Phillips (Shearsman, 2024; £12.95)

Plate tectonics

Elaine Randell is an English answer to Charles Olson – a kindred spirit with the poets of the *English Intelligencer*, the adventurous little magazine that began life on JH Prynne's college Xerox machine in the 1960s. There are at least two aspects to being an English Olsonian: one a free-versey tumbling form where it looks like prose with sudden indents for a whole block. The other is a strong interest in one's local settlement, and a general interest in plate tectonics and the history of landscape, the knowledge that we were all once on one continuous landmass. Near Romney Marsh, where Randell has lived for nearly 50 years, there was once a continuous connection to France that became flooded by the North Sea.

In the early 1980s she started publishing work that oddly anticipates the Conceptual Poetry movement around Kenneth Goldsmith, where there is a lot of hardly altered documentary material drawing on her professional life intervening in child custody and family breakdown cases, with extreme poverty nearly always the background. This technique is often described as Objectivist, but it isn't really like (say) Charles Reznikoff, for whose 'found' poetry that word was coined – Randell is something else entirely.

Randell often works lines from other writers into her poems, in quote marks. Each section of 'The Path Between the Yew Trees With Grass and Damp With Dew', for instance, begins with a line from Peter Ackroyd's novel *The Last Testament of Oscar Wilde*. Here's the first:

'The simplest lessons are those which are taught last.'

Often by those we least consider.
Humour.
The sun goes down on our minor
squalls and makes rainbows of our fears.
Illness.
Rest. The sleeping willow does not
ask for water waits for rain.
You won't be as you are now again.

This is not like the usual practice of adding an epigraph or an 'after' to a poem. Randell's quotes – often from other poems – are elusive, and only erratically documented; it is as if, by a different plate tectonics, her work was once part of the same terrain as theirs, and she is still sounding across. ❦ IL

Collected Poems & Prose by Elaine Randell (Shearsman, 2024; £22.95)

World without edge

A list of 'un-' words in Gillian Allnutt's new collection, *lode: unforgiving, unfit, untold, undaunted, unassimilable, unspent, unusual, unassuming, uncertain, unheard, uncompromising, unself-aware, un-/witting, unburied, unbelonging, unapprehended, unhalfbricking, unturned, unconfined, unknown.*

Allnutt's power is in her restraint. Her poetry, like the river in Corbridge, is 'intent, contained. // A listening in the rain'. Her work is a cutting away from everything that could be said, leaving the reader with a starting point rather than a done deed. Her use of form is unshowy ('Flame-thrower', for example, navigates end-stopping and enjambing in such a way that it only gradually announces itself a sestina). Rhymes and half-rhymes are frequent, but, rather than being imposed, they seem to come up from below the surface of a thought that was already there.

Particularly in 'Postwar', the book's opening section, Allnutt is concerned with what cannot be spoken of, 'the told and the untold pain'. The poet's father, who served among the arsenal of flame-throwing tanks that burned Belsen to the ground after its liberation, recurs throughout this section as he has in her previous work. Like the poet's own style, he is characterised by withholding: 'In silence somehow he would ask me to forgive his suffering'. From the unspeakable anguish of the 20th century and its dispossessed, we next arrive at the recent past of Covid lockdowns in the book's middle section. Allnutt matter-of-factly evokes a time in which our modes of communication were radically altered (Zoom makes an appearance); a time, for some, of solitude without speaking of any kind. A spider is 'woven into the wherewithal / Of her own imagination'; Allnutt also looks inward, with anchorite intensity.

Imagination in *lode* is indwelling (to use the title of a previous Allnutt collection); but it is also unbounded. An 'un-' word means freedom from definition, narrowing focus by saying what something is not, without being committed positively to naming what it is. 'Earth-hoard', the last of the book's three sections, reaches into the mysteries of nature and of the spirit, asking in the words of Julian of Norwich: 'Wouldst thou witten thy Lord's meaning in this thing?' Throughout we feel the potential of what has not yet been said: the 'hoard unheard'. Allnutt's negatives are not deadening but rather quickening to the imagination. The last line of verse in the collection is 'World without edge'; a fresh doxology for a still unknowable modern world, and the perfect final note for a quietly boundless collection that confirms Allnutt as one of the best English poets writing today. ❦ **MAC**

lode by Gillian Allnutt (Bloodaxe Books, 2025; £12)

Britain's rustbelt

Here is a handsomely printed and researched but rather hard to find new anthology, *Arcadian Rustbelt: The Second Generation of British Underground Poetry*, edited by Andrew Duncan and John Goodby. It is not definitive but introductory, and represents not a group position but a generation with some common forebears and reading, and dislikes. That generation is defined in the blurb as having 'emerged after 1980 but before 1994'; there are almost 300 pages of poems by – among others – DS Marriott, Khaled Hakim, Rod Mengham, Harry Gilonis and the editors themselves.

For some bearings, I would recommend to the general reader the now ancient anthology *A Various Art* (1987), which gathered together work by JH Prynne, Iain Sinclair and Victoria Forrest-Thompson. Where that earlier anthology had the shock of the new, *Arcadian Rustbelt* has some consolidation in pockets.

The editors gloss their title as evoking the limited idealism you can muster in an abandoned industrial estate. But the more common meaning of rust belt is American territory from a bit east of Chicago to just west of New York. It's blue-collar, and priced out of Manhattan dandyland (which would be, in anthology terms, Donald Allen's *New American Poetry 1945-60*).

Similarly pushed to the margins, work in this post-anthology-anthology smears traces of the *A Various Art* generation into the outwash: here bleached Prynnism, there more sweary and snarly Riley or Raworth.

The absolute standout for me was Frances Presley, and in a short review of a long hydra of heads and tails I'll give an example, to see some of the intrigue going for the centre ripple:

Retinal holes are sealed by applying buckles to the wall of the eye
which cause a scar reaction. A gas bubble holds the retina in position
until the reaction occurs. The bubble floats inside the eye cavity. As
the bubble begins to disperse, you will notice a line in your vision
that moves, similar to a spirit level. You will be able to see
above the line, but under the line the vision will be
fuzzy or blurred. The gas will eventually disperse
until it is only a small bubble at the
bottom of your eye which
will disappear too

❧ IL

Arcadian Rustbelt: The Second Generation of British Underground Poetry, ed Andrew Duncan and John Goodby
(Waterloo Press, 2024; £12)

Down with quarks, up with McVitie's!

I never expected be excited by Thornhill Park and Ride. Helen Farish was new to me when I heard her read at the TS Eliot Prize in January. It was an evening heavy with long abstract poems and space-jargon thrown on like edible glitter. (The reader might not need to know the precise meaning of – as a hypothetical example – 'quark' to enjoy it in a poem, but we should be convinced the *poet* knows.) When Farish's poems came driving down recognisable roads, in a world filled with Levi's and McVitie's, they were a relief. Here were poems with a sense of solidity, magnificently real.

The Penny Dropping pitches itself as about a 'cherished relationship from first meetings to eventual break-up' and this is almost true. It charts a love story from a meeting in Marrakesh far beyond the break-up, on to a lifetime of mourning and reflection. The relationship is only part of the story; this is a book about aging, and how memories are continuously overwritten.

A book that reminds us that acceptance is itself a kind of loss, since it marks the demise of a younger self that refused to accept.

It opens with the lovers meeting in a section that feels like a perpetual holiday: travelling in Morocco, living in Italy. When we jump abruptly to Oxford, where they split up, both speaker and reader are left wondering, 'what had happened to the undomesticated me / you'd fallen for'. This is followed by an aftermath which never ends. This linear timeline feels chosen to mock the very idea of chronological storytelling. From their first meeting the ending is foreshadowed, 'Did you observe / on that first full day together how I could flip? / Confident then crumbling'.

What most surprised me were the later poems considering taboos about loss. This is a relationship which ran through the speaker's 20s and 30s; they are now in their 60s. In 'The Joke', we learn she still carries her lost love's photo with her when she travels. She notes how 'The cleaning staff are so kind to me',

> ...and then it occurs to me —
> on top of the pile of books in my room
> they've seen your photo and they think,
> 'Her son, how handsome, and she keeps
> his photo with her, God willing he isn't dead,'

Here is the bravery of the book. We live in a world where a widow can mourn, and a divorcee is supposed to be… what? mournful and angry? But the unmarried woman whose relationship has broken up is expected to move on. To get back on the horse. Put herself back out there. This book refuses that expectation. ❦ **HH**

The Penny Dropping by Helen Farish (Bloodaxe Books, 2024; £12)

Key to contributors

❦ **AB: Ahana Banerji** studies English at Cambridge. Alongside her debut pamphlet *Piecemeal*, her work features in *Oxford Poetry* and *The White Review*. ❦ **AK: Anja Konig** grew up in the German language and now writes in English. Her first full collection *Animal Experiments* was nominated for the Laurel Prize. ❦ **AP: Anon.** ❦ **AS: Andrew Sclater** is 75, from Edinburgh, lives in Paris, and has written poetry all his adult life. His new pamphlet is due this autumn. ❦ **AW: Alex Wong** is the author of two collections, *Poems Without Irony* and *Shadow and Refrain*. ❦ **BP: Ben Philipps** lives in Oxford. ❦ **CE: Carrie Etter**'s latest collection is *Grief's Alphabet*. Her new pamphlet *Veer, Oscillate, Rest* is out now. ❦ **DF: Deborah Finding** is the author of *Vigils For Dead and Dying Girls* and *Amortisation*. She was the first poet-in-residence at the Soho Poly. ❦ **DS: Dan Sperrin.** ❦ **DW: David Wheatley** is the author of *Child Ballad*. He lives in rural Aberdeenshire. ❦ **EY: Eric Yip** is from Hong Kong and the author of *Exposure*. ❦ **FL: Fran Lock** is a poet, essayist, editor, and dog parent. She is the author of 14 poetry collections and numerous pamphlets. She lives in Kent. ❦ **GR: Graeme Richardson** is the *Sunday Times* poetry critic. His latest pamphlet is *Last of the Coalmine Choirboys*. ❦ **HC: Harry Cochrane** lives in Florence. ❦ **HG: Harry Gunston** is an English graduate student at Cambridge whose writing can be found in *Cambridge Review of Books*. ❦ **HH: Holly Hopkins**'s collection *The English Summer* was shortlisted for a Forward Prize, Seamus Heaney Prize, and Laurel Prize, and named a *Guardian* book of the year. ❦ **HT: Harriet Truscott** has never been to Rome. ❦ **IL: Ira Lightman** doesn't Disrupt / law / to schtup / for // tune stirs / stiff, harks / wealthier's / pock // et al / lows pit / pony haul. / Racket // of sad / ist blade. ❦ **JBR: Jacob Burgess Rollo**'s poetry features in *Fourteen Poems*, *Outcrop Poetry* and others. He was commended in *TPW*'s Poetry Prize 2025. ❦ **JMC: John McCullough**'s collection *Reckless Paper Birds* won the 2020 Hawthornden Prize for Literature. His latest book of poems is *Panic Response*. ❦ **JI: Jennifer Ingleheart** is Professor of Latin at

Durham University. Her *Masculine Plural* was a study of WWI poet Philip Gillespie Bainbrigge. ❧ **JN: Jack Nicholls**'s work appears in *The Poetry Review*, *PN Review* and *The New Statesman*. From Cornwall, he lives in Manchester. ❧ **JW: Joe Wright** is a poet from the North Pennines. He studies at Magdalene College, Cambridge. ❧ **JS: Jon Stone** edits books about monsters, ghosts, pirates, the moon and so on. ❧ **KS: Karen Solie** is from Saskatchewan. Her fifth collection, *The Caiplie Caves*, was shortlisted for the TS Eliot Prize. Her sixth collection, *Wellwater*, is out now. ❧ **LK: Luke Kennard** is a poet and novelist who teaches at the University of Birmingham. His seventh collection, *The Book of Jonah*, is out in October. ❧ **MA: Mona Arshi** trained as a Human Rights lawyer. Her debut *Small Hands* won a Forward Prize; her third collection, *Mouth*, is out in July. ❧ **MAC: Mary Anne Clark** is a caseworker in the charity sector. Her poetry pamphlet, *St*, came out in 2021. ❧ **MC: Martyn Crucefix** is the author of *Between a Drowning Man*; translations of Peter Huchel which won the 2020 Schlegel-Tieck Prize; and a Rilke selected, *Change Your Life*. ❧ **MF: Mark Fiddes** lives in the Middle East. He is winner of this year's Ledbury Prize and his third collection is *Other Saints Are Available*. ❧ **MG: Michael Grieve** lives and works in Fife. ❧ **MS: Maria Stepanova**, born in Moscow in 1972, is a poet, essayist and journalist. She left Russia after the full-scale invasion of Ukraine and now lives in exile in Europe. Her novel *In Memory of Memory* was shortlisted for the International Booker Prize, and her collection *Mädchen Ohne Kleider* (from which the poem in this issue is taken) won the Leipzig Book Award for European Understanding. ❧ **RMA: Anon.** ❧ **RMR: Rainer Maria Rilke** died in 1926, unfortunately. ❧ **SD: Sasha Dugdale** is a poet and translator. Her sixth book of poetry *The Strongbox* was published in 2024. ❧ **SHB: Sue Hyon Bae** is the author of *Truce Country*, translator of Ha Jaeyoun's *Radio Days*, and co-translator of Kim Hyesoon's *A Drink of Red Mirror*. ❧ **TD: Timothy Donnelly**'s most recent book is *Chariot*. His previous titles include *The Problem of the Many* and *The Cloud Corporation*. ❧ **TFS: Tristram Fane Saunders** is to blame for any errors in this magazine. ❧ **TY: Tamar Yoseloff**'s latest collection, *Belief Systems*, was a PBS recommendation. ❧ **VG: Vona Groarke**'s ninth poetry collection, *Infinity Pool*, is out in May. ❧ **WS: Will Staveley**'s poetry has been featured in over 20 journals. He writes for wherever will have him, which mainly means his own Substack.

In Issue No. 2:

❦ In the bath with Sylvia Plath

❦ Possum-hunting: the mischief of TS Eliot

❦ Mr Bones resurrected: Shane McCrae on John Berryman's unpublished *Dream Songs*

❦ New writing by Declan Ryan, Abigail Parry, Ian Duhig, Rishi Dastidar & Anthony Madrid